SECOND EDITION

Accounting 2000
Exercises

DON NOSEWORTHY

HESSER COLLEGE

PEARSON
PUBLISHING SOLUTIONS

Cover Art: "Reflections No. 2," by Angela Sciaraffa.

Printed in the United States of America

10 9 8 7 6 5 4 3 2 1

Please visit our website at www.sscp.com.

ISBN 0–536–02171–6

BA 98784

PEARSON PUBLISHING SOLUTIONS
160 Gould Street/Needham Heights, MA 02494
A Pearson Education Company

CONTENTS

Introduction

ACROSS

1 Number of closing entries
3 Initials of rules for accounting
9 Paper representing transaction
10 Cartoon guide through accounting
11 Book of final entry

DOWN

1 Time to complete accounting cycle
2 Third financial statement
4 Determine what something represents
5 Series of accounting steps
6 The language of accounting
7 Sorting and summarizing
8 Book of original entry
12 Write results of analyzing

EXERCISES

CHAPTER 1

Starting Our Business

ACROSS

3 Items that can be owned
6 The accounting equation must do this
9 What a business earns

DOWN

1 Amounts owed outside the business
2 Charge expenses as they are incurred
4 Costs incurred to run the business
5 What the owner is worth in the business
7 Recording when earned or incurred
8 What the owner puts into the business

Chapter One

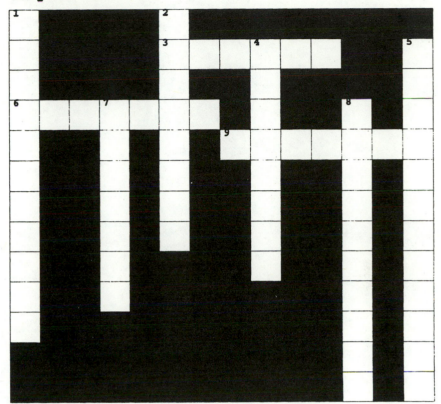

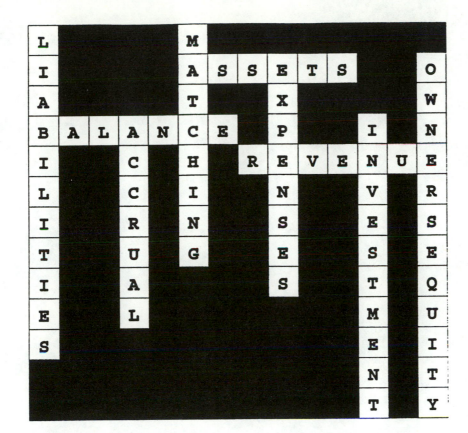

ISDO™ SELF √ PRACTICE QUIZ 1

The Accounting Cycle

CIRCLE YOUR CHOICE!

1. Which of the following best describes accounting?

   A. diary   B. book   C. directory   D. list

2. How many steps are there in our accounting cycle?

   A. 8   B. 6   C. 9   D. 3

3. What does the word analyze mean?

   A. ignore   B. examine   C. write down   D. list

4. Which word most closely describes a business transaction?

   A. pilfer   B. exchange   C. cash   D. in

5. Which of the following most closely describes what occurs in a business transaction?

   A. up/down   B. over/under   c. in/out   D. go/stay

6. Which of the following are entries first written in?

   A. ledger   B. checkbook   C. receipt book   D. journal

7. The process of sorting and summarizing gives need for which additional book?

   A. ledger   B. checkbook   C. receipt book   D. journal

8. Sorting and summarizing accounting information is called:

   A. journalizing   B. posting   C. copying   D. plagiarism

9. Which of the following best describes revenue?

   A. what is received   B. what is taken in   C. what is earned   D. what is collected

10. Which of the following best describes an expense?

    A. what goes out   B. what is paid   C. costs incurred to run the business   D. money that is paid to others

CHAPTER ONE

STARTING OUR BUSINESS

EXERCISES

Characteristics of Sole Proprietorships

Ex. 1. Which of the following are characteristics of the sole proprietorship form of business organization? If the characteristic does apply to a sole proprietorship, is it considered to be an advantage or a disadvantage?

	Yes	No		Adv.	Disad
a. The owner's equity of the company is divided into shares of stock.					
b. The owner is personally liable for all the debts of the business.					
c. The business is subject to much governmental control.					
d. All the profits belong to the owner.					
e. All the losses must be absorbed by the owner.					
f. The amount of capital available to operate the business may be limited.					
g. Permission must be received from the state to start and end the business.					
h. The decision making responsibility belongs to the owner.					
i. A serious time commitment is required by the owner.					
j. There must be at least two owners of the business.					

Account Identification

Ex. 2.   Identify each of the following accounts that a business could use as an asset, liability, or part of owner's equity.

Cash	_____	Notes Payable	_____
Accounts Payable	_____	Prepaid Insurance	_____
Rent Expense	_____	Prepaid Rent	_____
Supplies	_____	Insurance Expense	_____
Accounts Receivable	_____	Capital	_____
Fees Earned	_____	Utility Expense	_____
Office Equipment	_____	Automobile	_____
Taxes Payable	_____	Automobile Cleaning	
Salary Expense	_____	Expense	_____
Drawing	_____	Dry Cleaning Expense	_____
		Depreciation Expense	_____

Positive and Negative Equity Accounts

Ex. 3.   For the accounts in Exercise 2 that were identified as owner's equity, state which are positive equity and which are negative equity accounts.

Positive   **Negative**

The Accounting Equation

Ex. 4.   Determine the missing amounts in the accounting equation below:

	Assets	=	Liabilities	+	Owner's Equity
a.			$12,000		$13,000
b.	$80,000				$40,000
c.	$35,000		$17,000		

Owner's Equity Transactions

Ex. 5. Which of the following business transactions affect owner's equity? If the transaction does affect owner's equity, state whether the effect is positive or negative.

Transaction	+	–	No Effect
a. Owner invested cash into the business.			
b. Bought supplies for cash.			
c. Bought supplies on account.			
d. Used supplies in the operation of the business.			
e. Owner withdrew cash for personal use.			
f. Paid an amount owed to a creditor.			
g. Received cash from what we are in business for.			
h. Sold some of our excess office equipment that was no longer needed by the business. It was sold for what it was worth.			
i. Borrowed money from a bank.			
j. Paid the bank interest on the amount borrowed in i.			

Transactions and How They Affect the Accounting Equation

Ex. 6. Give an example of a transaction that would create the described effect on the accounting equation.

a. Increase an asset and increase owner's equity.

b. Increase an asset and decrease an asset.

c. Increase an asset and increase a liability.

d. Decrease an asset and decrease a liability.

e. Decrease an asset and decrease owner's equity.

f. Increase a liability and decrease owner's equity.

Transactions and How They Affect the Accounting Equation

Ex. 7.   Identify how the following business transactions affect the accounting equation. If the transaction causes an increase place a +, or if it causes a decrease place a – in the appropriate space. Remember in your analysis that each transaction must affect at least two things. Your analysis can result in two increases, two decreases, or one of each. It also can involve any combination of the classifications of accounts.

If the transaction creates revenue or causes an expense to be incurred, indicate the effect of the transaction on the net income of the business.

Transaction	Asset	Liability	Owner's Equity	Net Income
a. Owner invests cash into business.				
b. Buy supplies on account.				
c. Buy office equipment for cash.				
d. Sell services and receive cash.				
e. Collect an account receivable.				
f. Owner withdraws cash from business.				
g. Paid wages with cash to employee.				
h. Sell services of the business on credit.				
i. Borrow cash to be paid back later.				
j. Use supplies in the running of the business.				
k. Bought delivery truck. Paid cash for part and agreed to pay the rest at a later date.				
l. Returned some of the supplies bought on account in letter b.				

Calculation of Net Income

Ex. 8.   A business had the following balances in its asset and liability accounts at the beginning and end of the current fiscal period:

	Assets	Liabilities
Beginning of the fiscal period	$100,000	$20,000
End of the fiscal period	180,000	60,000

Determine the amount of the net income or net loss for the fiscal period under each of the following independent situations:

a.   The owner made no additional investments and made no withdrawals.

b.   The owner made an investment of $10,000 but made no withdrawals.

c.   The owner made no investments but made a withdrawal of $5,000.

d.   The owner made an investment of $20,000 and a withdrawal of $25,000.

NOTES

NOTES

NOTES

WORKPAPER FOR EXERCISES

EXERCISES

CHAPTER 2

**Debit, Debit, Debit,
Credit, Credit, Credit**

Chapter Two

ACROSS

5 Number of events affecting owner's worth

9 Amount owed the business from outside

DOWN

1 Determined by side found on in equation

2 Each entry has a debit and a credit

3 Left

4 Account used for anaylzing

6 Person or company money is owed to

7 More than one debit - credit in entry

8 Right

10 Owner's equity accounts are this

CHAPTER TWO

DEBIT, DEBIT, DEBIT, CREDIT, CREDIT, CREDIT

EXERCISES

What Is Revenue?

Ex. 1. Which of the following business transactions would create revenue for a business? If a transaction does not create revenue, explain why.

    a. The owner puts $30,000 of their own cash into the business.

    b. Provided $600 of professional services to clients on credit.

    c. Collected $400 of the money owed from letter b.

    d. Received $900 cash for professional services to be provided in the next fiscal period.

    e. Borrowed $1,000 from the bank for use in the business.

What Is An Expense?

Ex. 2. Which of the following business transactions would cause an expense to have been incurred for the business? If the transaction does not involve an expense, explain why.

    a. Paid $200 on balance due to a creditor.

    b. Paid $500 salary to the office receptionist.

    c. Paid $600 for office equipment.

    d. The owner withdrew $100 for show tickets.

    e. Paid the utility bill of $150.

Analyzing With Debits and Credits

Ex. 3. Using the transactions given below, determine what account would require a debit and what account would require a credit to correctly analyze the exchange taking place. T accounts with the account titles needed for the analysis have been provided. When determining which accounts will be debited and credited:

1. Identify the account as an asset, liability, or part of owner's equity.

2. Determine whether the account has a normal debit or credit balance based on its location in the accounting equation.

3. If the account is part of owner's equity, identify it as either positive or negative equity.

4. Based on your analysis, indicate the required Dr. and Cr.

Remember: **ASSETS = LIABILITIES + OWNER'S EQUITY**
DEBIT means **LEFT**   **CREDIT** means **RIGHT**

Increase
Same side
Decrease
Opposite side
™

THE ACCOUNT TO BE DEBITED IS NOT NECESSARILY THE FIRST LISTED.

The first transaction is presented as an example:

a. The owner made an investment of $5,000 cash into the business.

CASH(A) DR		CAPITAL(OE) CR	
5000			5000

b. Bought $400 of supplies on account.

SUPPLIES		ACCOUNTS PAYABLE	

(Continued)

c.   Bought land for $7,000.

CASH	LAND

d.   Paid $200 to creditors on account.

CASH	ACCOUNTS PAYABLE

e.   The owner withdrew $50 cash from the business.

DRAWING	CASH

f.   Paid the rent for the month, $900.

CASH	RENT EXPENSE

g.   We earned and received $100 in cash for doing our job.

SERVICE INCOME	CASH

h.   We earned $200 from doing our job but will receive the money later.

ACCOUNTS RECEIVABLE	SERVICE INCOME

i.   We collected the $200 that was owed us.

ACCOUNTS RECEIVABLE	CASH

(Continued)

j.   We used $30 of supplies in the operation of the business.

<u>   SUPPLIES   </u>   <u>SUPPLIES EXPENSE</u>

Balance Sides, Increase Sides, and Decrease Sides

Ex. 4.   Using the T accounts given below, do or answer the following:

    a.   Indicate the debit side and the credit side of each account by writing Dr. or Cr. on the appropriate side.

    b.   Indicate which is the normal balance side of each account by writing BAL. on the appropriate side. If the account is part of owner's equity, put BAL. on the side showing the effect, either positive or negative, it has on the owner's worth.

    c.   Indicate which side of the account is used for increases (+) and for decreases (–). If the account is part of owner's equity, write the word ALWAYS on the side indicated by your answer to part b.

    d.   Which of the accounts would normally have amounts placed on **either** the debit or credit side during the analysis of transactions?

    e.   Which of the accounts would normally have amounts placed on **only** the debit or the credit side during the analysis of transactions?

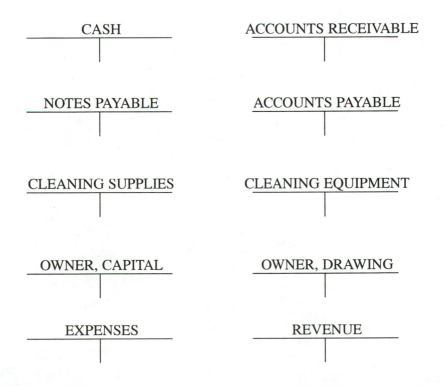

Classification of Accounts and Their Balances

Ex. 5. Indicate whether the following accounts are assets, liabilities, or part of owner's equity. If the account is part of owner's equity, indicate whether it is positive or negative equity. After identifying the classification of an account, indicate whether the normal balance is a debit (Dr.) or credit (Cr). If the account is part of owner's equity, indicate its balance as it affects what the owner of the business is worth and write the word ALWAYS preceding the appropriate response.

ACCOUNT	TYPE		NORMAL OR ALWAYS BALANCE
0. RENT EXPENSE	OE —	ALWAYS	DR
1. ACCOUNTS PAYABLE			
2. ACCOUNTS RECEIVABLE			
3. ADVERTISING EXPENSE			
4. BUILDINGS			
5. OWNER'S CAPITAL			
6. DELIVERY EQUIPMENT			
7. DEPRECIATION EXPENSE			
8. OWNER'S DRAWING			
9. FEES EARNED	OE		+ CR
10. INSURANCE EXPENSE	OE		- DEBIT
11. INTEREST PAYABLE	Liability		
12. LAND	A		
13. MACHINERY	A		
14. MORTGAGE PAYABLE	Liab		
15. NOTE PAYABLE (30 DAYS)	Liab		
16. NOTE PAYABLE (5 MONTHS)	Liab		
17. NOTES RECEIVABLE	A		
18. PREPAID INSURANCE	A		+
19. SALARIES PAYABLE	Liability		

(Continued)

20. PREPAID RENT   *A*   _____

21. STORE SUPPLIES   *A*   _____

22. SUPPLIES EXPENSE   *A*   *-Debit*

23. TAXES PAYABLE   *Liability*

24. UTILITIES EXPENSE   *OE*   *-Debit*

25. COMMISSIONS EARNED   *OE*   *+Credit*

Transaction Analysis With T Accounts

Ex. 6. The Jones Company is an Interior Design Company organized in Monterey, California. Using the following chart of accounts, complete the following:

1. Determine the accounts affected and label a T account for each using the account titles in the chart of accounts.

2. Identify the account as an asset, liability, or owner's equity.

3. Indicate the normal balance of the account based on its location in the accounting equation. If the account is part of owner's equity, indicate whether it is positive or negative equity.

4. Based on your analysis, record the appropriate Dr. and Cr.

CHART OF ACCOUNTS

CASH	MR. JONES, CAPITAL
OFFICE SUPPLIES	MR. JONES, DRAWING
ACCOUNTS RECEIVABLE	INTERIOR DESIGN REVENUE
OFFICE EQUIPMENT	ADVERTISING EXPENSE
ACCOUNTS PAYABLE	SALARY EXPENSE
	SUPPLIES EXPENSE

The first transaction is given as an example:

July 1. Mr. Jones invested $80,000 cash into his business.

MR. JONES, CAPITAL (OE)	CASH (A)
80000	80000

(Continued)

2. Jones Company bought office equipment on account, $4,000.

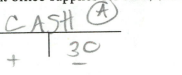 office Equipment (A)
```
4000 |
  +    _
```
Accounts payable (L)
```
     | 4000
  -  |  +
```

4. Bought office supplies for cash, $30.

CASH (A)
```
     |  30
  +  |  _
```
office Supplies (A)
```
 30  |
  +  |  _
```

6. Paid $85 for an advertisement in the local newspaper.

CASH (A)
```
     |  80
  +  |  _
```
Adv. Expense (OE)
```
 85  |
  _  |  +
```

8. Received interior design revenue from cash customer, $1,400.

CASH (A)
```
1,400 |
  +   |  _
```
Interior Design REV (OE)
```
1,400 | 1,400
  _   |  +
```

12. Charged customers for interior design services provided on account, $2,500.

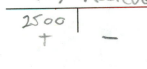 Interior Design REV (OE)
```
     | 2500
     |  +
```
A / Recievable (A)
```
2500 |
  +  |  _
```

15. Paid $2,800 to creditors on account.

CASH (A)
```
     | 2800
  +  |  _
```
Accounts Payable (L)
```
2800 |
  _  |  +
```

19. Received $2,500 owed us from the 12th.

Accounts Recievable (A)
```
     | 2500
  +  |  _
```
CASH (A)
```
2500 |
  +  |  _
```

23. Paid the salaries for the month, $1,500.

CASH (A)
```
     | 1500
  +  |  _
```
Salaries Expense (OE)
```
1500 |
  _  |  +
```
(Continued)

25. Mr. Jones, owner, withdrew $3,000 cash for personal use.

withdrawing (OE)
3000 |
   −   +

CASH (A)
      | 3000
  ⊥   −

31. Recorded the use of $25 of office supplies for the month.

office suplies (A)
      | 25
  +   −

supplies Expense (OE)
 25 |
   −   +

Ex. 7. This Exercise must be completed before Exercise 1 in Chapter 3 is assigned.

Using the following accounts:

CASH   ACCOUNTS PAYABLE
SUPPLIES   J. SMITH, CAPITAL
ACCOUNTS RECEIVABLE   J. SMITH, DRAWING
EQUIPMENT   INCOME
LAND   SALARY EXPENSE
                            SUPPLIES EXPENSE

Record the following transactions in the "T" accounts provided.

Remember: **ASSETS = LIABILITIES + OWNER'S EQUITY**
  − DEBIT means **LEFT**   **+CREDIT** means **RIGHT**

1. John Smith, owner, invested $1,000 cash into his business.

CASH (A)
      | 1000
  +   −

J. Smith, Capital (OE)
      | 1000
  −   +

2. Bought supplies for cash, $200.

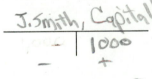

CASH (A)
      | 200
  +   −

Supplies (A)
 200 |
  +   −

3. Bought equipment on account, $4,000.

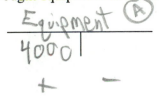

Equipment (A)
4000 |
  +   −

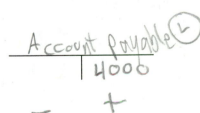

Account payable (L)
      | 4000
  −   +

(Continued)

4. Paid for the above (#3) equipment that had been bought on account.

CASH Ⓐ		Account Payable Ⓛ	
	4000	4000	
+	−	−	+

5. John Smith, owner, withdrew $300 from the business.

 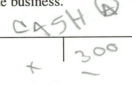

J Smith withdrawing ⓄⒺ		CASH Ⓐ	
300			300
−	+	+	−

6. The business paid salaries of $450.

Salaries Exp ⓄⒺ		CASH Ⓐ	
450			450
−	+	+	−

7. The business received cash, $200, from what they are in business for. (Income)

Income ⓄⒺ		CASH Ⓐ	
	200	200	
−	+	+	−

8. The business performed its service on account, $480, and will collect the cash at a later date. Ⓐ

Income ⓄⒺ		Accounts Recievable Ⓐ	
450	450	480	
−	+	+	−

9. We received the $480 cash owed us from transaction #8.

CASH Ⓐ		Accounts recievable Ⓐ	
480			480
+	−	+	

10. The business bought land for $50,000. It paid $30,000 cash immediately and promised to pay the balance within the next month. **THIS IS CALLED A COMPOUND ENTRY AS IT CONTAINS MORE THAN 2 ACCOUNTS.**

LAND Ⓐ		CASH Ⓐ	
50,000			30,000
+	−	+	−

Accounts Payable Ⓛ	
	20,000
−	+

NOTES

WORKPAPER FOR EXERCISES

WORKPAPER FOR EXERCISES

EXERCISES

CHAPTER 3

Journalizing, Posting and Trial Balance

Chapter Three

ACROSS

3 Revenues begin with this number
4 Where all the accounts are found
5 Trial balance does not provide this 100%
7 Liabilities begin with this number
9 Transfer from journal to ledger
11 Assets begin with this number
13 Equity begins with this number
15 Drawn to show addition or subtraction
16 Done to numbers that are alike

DOWN

1 Reversing two numbers
2 List of all the accounts in the business
6 Expenses begin with this number
8 Drawn to show work is done
10 Enter information into a journal
12 Found in the general ledger
14 Adding or deleting a 0

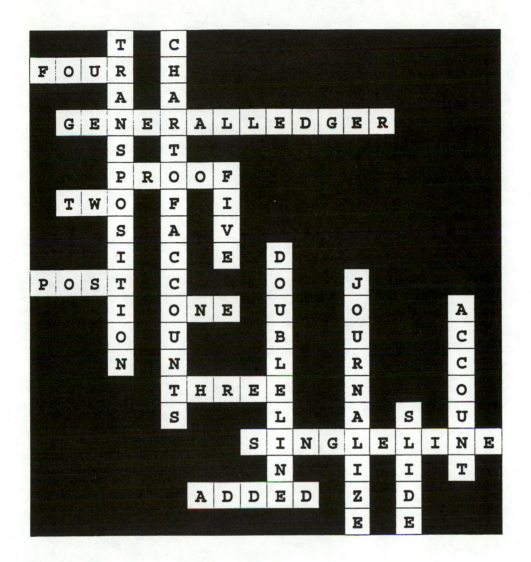

CHAPTER THREE

JOURNALIZING, POSTING, AND TRIAL BALANCE

EXERCISES

Journalizing Transactions

Ex. 1.   Using the results from the analysis of the transactions in Exercise 7 of Chapter 2, record the journal entries required. Be sure to follow the correct journalizing procedures outlined and discussed in Chapter 3 of your textbook.

GENERAL JOURNAL   PAGE 1

Date	Description	P.R.	Debit	Credit

(Continued)

GENERAL JOURNAL

Date	Description	P.R.	Debit	Credit

Basic Posting

Ex. 2. Today you will learn the skill of posting. **Posting** means the systematic transfer of information from the journal to ledger. There are *four* steps in this basic posting procedure. *They must be followed in the correct order*. These steps are:

1. Copy the date of the transaction from the journal into the date column of the appropriate account in the ledger.

2. Copy the page number of the journal into the posting reference column of the account in the ledger.

3. Transfer the amount to be posted from the journal into its "new home" in the amount column of the appropriate account.

4. Your posting is completed by bringing the number of the account in the ledger back to the posting reference column of the journal.

GENERAL JOURNAL   PAGE 4

DATE	ACCOUNT TITLE	P.R.	DEBIT	CREDIT
Oct 1	Supplies		800 00	
	Cash			800 00
2	Cash		1000 00	
	John Smith, Capital			1000 00

GENERAL LEDGER

Cash   11

DATE	PR	AMT	DATE	PR	AMT

Supplies   12

DATE	PR	AMT	DATE	PR	AMT

John Smith, Capital   31

DATE	PR	AMT	DATE	PR	AMT

Four-Column Balance Account Posting

Ex. 3. Advantages:

1. Always current balance.

2. No pencil footings needed.

Guiding Rules:

If the amounts you are working with are **ALIKE—ADD THEM** to calculate the new balance.

If the amounts you are working with are **NOT ALIKE—SUBTRACT THEM** to calculate the new balance. If the larger number in the subtraction process is a debit—*the new balance will also be a debit*. If the larger number in the subtraction process is a credit—*the new balance will be a credit.* Once a balance is established, it will never "go" to the other side; i.e., a debit balance will always continue down the **DR. BAL**. column.

This means if you have a **DR/DR—ADD THEM**; if you have a **CR/CR—ADD THEM** but if you have a **DR/CR** or **CR/DR** combination you would **SUBTRACT THEM** to find the balance of your account. See rule in above paragraph.

PRACTICE ON THE FOLLOWING ILLUSTRATION:

Post the following amounts from *Page 9* of the general journal to the cash account provided. The journal provided is not a complete journal!

Post Ref

Oct.	1.	$9000 Dr.
	3.	800 Dr
	5.	1000 Cr.
	7.	600 Dr.
	8.	500 Cr.
	31.	100 Dr.

CASH   11

DATE	DESCRIPTION	P.R.	DEBIT	CREDIT	DR.BAL	CR.BAL

As you have seen, as cash is an asset (**DR. BAL**) *the credit balance column was never used*. With accounts payable (**CR. BAL**) the **DR. Bal** column would never the used.

Journalizing, Posting, and Preparing a Trial Balance

Ex. 4. During the current year, I. M. Rich started the Rich Service Company.

1. Record the following transactions in the two-column general journal provided.

September   1.   Mr. Rich invested $5,000 in cash, equipment worth $20,000 and a vehicle costing $15,000 into his business. (COMPOUND ENTRY)

16.   Mr. Rich bought additional equipment costing $4,000. It will be paid for at a later date as it was bought on account.

29.   Mr. Rich paid his creditors $3,000 of what he owed them on account.

2. Post to the appropriate ledger accounts provided.

3. Prepare a trial balance using the form at the bottom of the next page.

GENERAL JOURNAL
PAGE 1

DATE		DESCRIPTION	P.R.	DEBIT	CREDIT

RICH COMPANY
TRIAL BALANCE
SEPTEMBER 30, 19_____   Debit   Credit

	Debit	Credit

GENERAL LEDGER ACCOUNTS

Cash   *Account No. 11*

DATE		ITEM	P.R.	DEBIT	CREDIT	DEBIT BAL.	CREDIT BAL.

Equipment   *Account No. 17*

DATE		ITEM	P.R.	DEBIT	CREDIT	DEBIT BAL.	CREDIT BAL.

Vehicles   *Account No. 18*

DATE		ITEM	P.R.	DEBIT	CREDIT	DEBIT BAL.	CREDIT BAL.

Accounts Payable   *Account No. 21*

DATE		ITEM	P.R.	DEBIT	CREDIT	DEBIT BAL.	CREDIT BAL.

I.M. Rich, Captial   *Account No. 31*

DATE		ITEM	P.R.	DEBIT	CREDIT	DEBIT BAL.	CREDIT BAL.

Journalizing, Posting, and Preparing a Trial Balance

Ex. 5.   Using the forms provided, a) record the following transactions in the general journal for Jones Talent Agency. Use only the accounts given below in their chart of accounts:

CASH   A. JONES, CAPITAL

ACCOUNTS RECEIVABLE   A. JONES, DRAWING

SUPPLIES   TALENT FEES EARNED

EQUIPMENT   WAGES EXPENSE

ACCOUNTS PAYABLE   TELEPHONE EXPENSE

                                                    ADVERTISING EXPENSE

FEB.   1.   A. Jones, owner, made an investment of $5,000 into her business.

              3.   Bought supplies for cash, $50.

              4.   Bought equipment on account from Nelson Company, $3,000.

              6.   Received cash from customer for providing them with talent for their convention, $750.

              13.   Provided talent for club meeting; $100. They will pay us later.

              17.   Paid the telephone bill, $20.

              23.   Paid the amount owed for the equipment bought on February 4, $3,000.

              26.   Received the money owed us from February 13, $100.

              26.   Paid $50 for newspaper advertisement.

              27.   A. Jones, owner, withdrew $500 cash for personal use.

              28.   Paid the wages of our employee, $250.

b.   Post the transactions to the appropriate accounts in the general ledger.

c.   Prepare a trial balance. The correct trial balance totals are $5,850. Good Luck!!

(Continued)

JONES TALENT AGENCY
GENERAL JOURNAL

PAGE 1

Date	Account Title and Description	P.R.	Debit	Credit

(Continued)

GENERAL LEDGER OF JONES TALENT AGENCY

CASH   ACCOUNT NO. 111

Date	Item	P.R.	Debit	Credit	Balance Debit	Balance Credit

ACCOUNTS RECEIVABLE   ACCOUNT NO. 113

Date	Item	P.R.	Debit	Credit	Balance Debit	Balance Credit

SUPPLIES   ACCOUNT NO. 131

Date	Item	P.R.	Debit	Credit	Balance Debit	Balance Credit

EQUIPMENT   ACCOUNT NO. 141

Date	Item	P.R.	Debit	Credit	Balance Debit	Balance Credit

(Continued)   **41**

ACCOUNTS PAYABLE   ACCOUNT NO. 211

Date	Item	P.R.	Debit	Credit	Balance	
					Debit	Credit

A. JONES, CAPITAL   ACCOUNT NO. 311

Date	Item	P.R.	Debit	Credit	Balance	
					Debit	Credit

A. JONES, DRAWING   ACCOUNT NO. 321

Date	Item	P.R.	Debit	Credit	Balance	
					Debit	Credit

TALENT FEES EARNED   ACCOUNT NO. 411

Date	Item	P.R.	Debit	Credit	Balance	
					Debit	Credit

(Continued)

WAGE EXPENSE
ACCOUNT NO. 511

Date	Item	P.R.	Debit	Credit	Balance	
					Debit	Credit

TELEPHONE EXPENSE
ACCOUNT NO. 521

Date	Item	P.R.	Debit	Credit	Balance	
					Debit	Credit

ADVERTISING EXPENSE
ACCOUNT NO. 531

Date	Item	P.R.	Debit	Credit	Balance	
					Debit	Credit

c) **TRIAL BALANCE** **DEBIT** **CREDIT**

	Debit	Credit

Journalizing, Posting, and Preparing a Trial Balance

Ex. 6. Miles Delivery Service began business on June 1 of the current year. During the month the following transactions were completed:

June

1. The owner, Miles Away, invested $10,000 in cash and a delivery truck with a fair market value of $12,000 into the business.

1. Paid the rent for June, $1,500.

1. Bought an insurance policy with an annual premium of $1,200.

3. Bought office equipment on account, $1,800.

3. Bought office supplies on account, $400.

5. Earned $3,000 in delivery fees for the week and received cash.

5. Earned $2,500 in delivery fees that will be collected later.

7. Paid $1,800 on account for the office equipment bought on June 3.

12. Received $1,700 on account from customers.

12. Received $2,300 in cash from delivery fees for the week.

15. Miles withdrew $1,500 from the business for personal use.

15. Paid salary of $1,300 to office manager.

18. Bought additional supplies for cash, $300.

25. Paid the telephone bill amounting to $110.

30. Paid the utility bill, $215.

30. Determined that office supplies totaling $500 had been used during the month.

30. One month's insurance premium amounting to $100 was used in the month of June.

Required:

a. Prepare general journal entries to record the above transactions. In recording the transactions use only the following accounts: Cash; Accounts Receivable; Office Supplies; Prepaid Insurance; Office Equipment; Delivery Truck; Accounts Payable; Miles Away, Capital; Miles Away, Drawing; Delivery Service Income; Rent Expense; Salary Expense; Insurance Expense; Supplies Expense; Telephone Expense; Utilities Expense.

b. Post the entries to the appropriate accounts in the general ledger updating balances when necessary.

c. Prepare a trial balance as of June 30.

(Continued)

Journal   **Page 1**

Date	Description	P.R.	Debit	Credit

(Continued)

Journal   Page 2

Date		Description	P.R.	Debit						Credit					

(Continued)

GENERAL LEDGER

CASH   ACCOUNT NO. 11

Date	Item	P.R.	Debit	Credit	Balance Debit	Balance Credit

ACCOUNTS RECEIVABLE   ACCOUNT NO. 12

Date	Item	P.R.	Debit	Credit	Balance Debit	Balance Credit

OFFICE SUPPLIES   ACCOUNT NO. 13

Date	Item	P.R.	Debit	Credit	Balance Debit	Balance Credit

PREPAID INSURANCE   ACCOUNT NO. 14

Date	Item	P.R.	Debit	Credit	Balance Debit	Balance Credit

(Continued)

OFFICE EQUIPMENT   ACCOUNT NO. 15

Date	Item	P.R.	Debit	Credit	Balance Debit	Balance Credit

DELIVERY TRUCK   ACCOUNT NO. 16

Date	Item	P.R.	Debit	Credit	Balance Debit	Balance Credit

ACCOUNTS PAYABLE   ACCOUNT NO. 21

Date	Item	P.R.	Debit	Credit	Balance Debit	Balance Credit

MILES AWAY, CAPITAL   ACCOUNT NO. 31

Date	Item	P.R.	Debit	Credit	Balance Debit	Balance Credit

MILES AWAY, DRAWING   ACCOUNT NO. 32

Date	Item	P.R.	Debit	Credit	Balance Debit	Balance Credit

(Continued)

DELIVERY SERVICE INCOME   ACCOUNT NO. 41

Date	Item	P.R.	Debit		Credit		Balance			
							Debit		Credit	

RENT EXPENSE   ACCOUNT NO. 51

Date	Item	P.R.	Debit		Credit		Balance			
							Debit		Credit	

SALARY EXPENSE   ACCOUNT NO. 52

Date	Item	P.R.	Debit		Credit		Balance			
							Debit		Credit	

INSURANCE EXPENSE   ACCOUNT NO. 53

Date	Item	P.R.	Debit		Credit		Balance			
							Debit		Credit	

SUPPLIES EXPENSE   ACCOUNT NO. 54

Date	Item	P.R.	Debit		Credit		Balance			
							Debit		Credit	

(Continued)   **49**

TELEPHONE EXPENSE   ACCOUNT NO. 55

Date	Item	P.R.	Debit	Credit	Balance Debit	Balance Credit

UTILITIES EXPENSE   ACCOUNT NO. 56

Date	Item	P.R.	Debit	Credit	Balance Debit	Balance Credit

c)

Miles Delivery Service
TRIAL BALANCE
June 30, _____

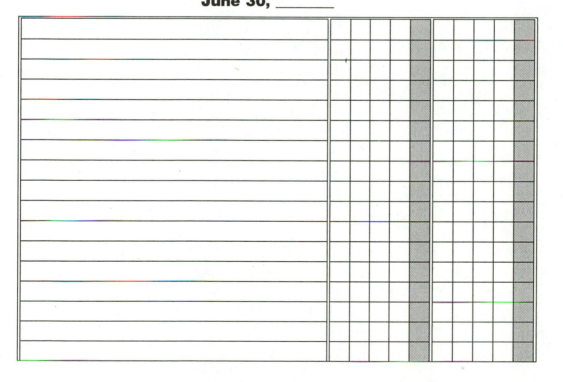

EXERCISES

CHAPTER 4

Basic Financial Statements

ACROSS

3 Third part of statement heading

8 Proves accounting equation balances

9 Amounts in right column of statements

10 Step five of accounting cycle

11 Second part of statement heading

12 Amounts in left column of statements

DOWN

1 Occurs when expenses exceed revenue

2 When statements rely on each other

4 Reports net income or net loss

5 Number of parts in statement heading

6 Occurs when revenue exceeds expenses

7 First part of statement heading

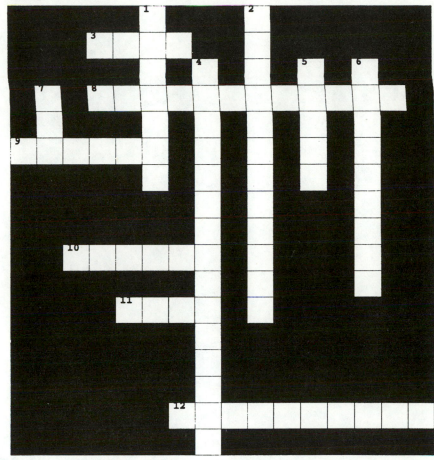

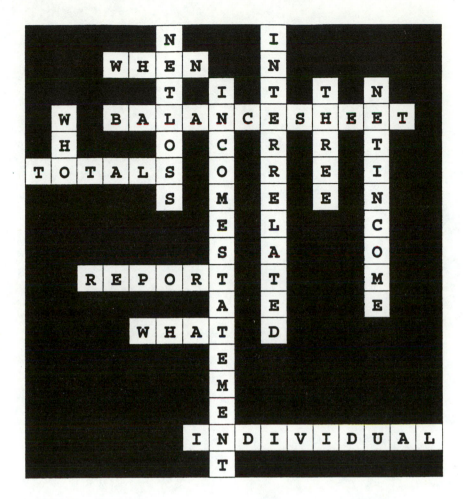

CHAPTER FOUR

BASIC FINANCIAL STATEMENTS

EXERCISES

Determining Which Financial Statement Accounts Appear On

Ex. 1.   Indicate whether the following accounts would appear on an income statement or a balance sheet: **use IS for income statement or BS for balance sheet.**

ACCOUNT	FINANCIAL STATEMENT
1. CASH	_____
2. ACCOUNTS PAYABLE	_____
3. ACCOUNTS RECEIVABLE	_____
4. ADVERTISING EXPENSE	_____
5. BUILDINGS	_____
6. OWNER'S CAPITAL	_____
7. DELIVERY EQUIPMENT	_____
8. DEPRECIATION EXPENSE	_____
9. OWNER'S DRAWING	_____
10. FEES EARNED	_____
11. INSURANCE EXPENSE	_____
12. INTEREST PAYABLE	_____
13. LAND	_____
14. MACHINERY	_____
15. MORTGAGE PAYABLE	_____
16. NOTES PAYABLE	_____
17. NOTES RECEIVABLE	_____
18. PREPAID INSURANCE	_____
19. COMMISSIONS EARNED	_____
20. STORE SUPPLIES	_____

Net Income Calculation

Ex. 2.   Miles Away is owner of the Miles Delivery Service. During the current month the following revenue was earned and expenses incurred:

Salary Expense	$4,000	Rent Expense	$1,000
Advertising Expense	800	Gasoline Expense	300
Delivery Fees	6,000	Miscellaneous Expense	100

Calculate the amount of net income or net loss for the month.

Determining Owner's Equity

Ex. 3.   Miles Away (Exercise 2) had a capital balance of $10,000 at the beginning of the month. During the month, Miles withdrew $2,000 for personal use. Using this information and the net income or net loss calculated in Exercise 2, determine what Miles owner's equity was in his business at the end of the month.

Financial Statement Identification

Ex. 4.   If all three basic financial statements are prepared, indicate whether the following items would appear on an income statement (IS), statement of owner's equity (OE), or a balance sheet (BS).

   a.   Cash received from customers.   _____

   b.   Rent expense incurred.   _____

   c.   Delivery fees earned.   _____

   d.   Office supplies.   _____

   e.   Investment of the owner.   _____

   f.   Accounts payable.   _____

   g.   Withdrawals made by the owner.   _____

Accounting Equation—Fill in the Missing Amounts

Ex. 5. Determine the missing amount in each of the following independent situations:

	a	b	c	d
Owner's Equity, Beginning	$3,000	$ 0	$ 0	$ 0
Owner's Investments	7000	?	8,000	5,000
Owner's Withdrawals	?	6,000	3,000	2,000
Net Income (Loss) for period	8,000	9,000	(2,000)	?
Owner's Equity, Ending	14,000	12,000	?	2,000

Basic Financial Statements

Ex. 6. R.U. Happy started a business on January 1 with an investment of $12,500. During the year he withdrew $11,850 for personal use.

The balances of the business assets, liabilities, and owner's equity at the end of the year, December 31, are as follows:

CASH	.$10,050
ACCOUNTS RECEIVABLE	.3,100
SUPPLIES	.1,200
ACCOUNTS PAYABLE	.2,150
SERVICE INCOME	.25,000
ADVERTISING EXPENSE	.4,000
RENTAL EXPENSE	.1,500
UTILITIES EXPENSE	.500
SUPPLIES EXPENSE	.6,100
MISCELLANEOUS EXPENSE	.1,350

Instructions: Using the forms provided, prepare the following:

a) An income statement for the current year.

b) A statement of owner's equity at the end of the current year.

c) A balance sheet as of December 31 of the current year.

(Continued)

R.U. HAPPY
INCOME STATEMENT
FOR THE CURRENT YEAR ENDED DECEMBER 31, _____

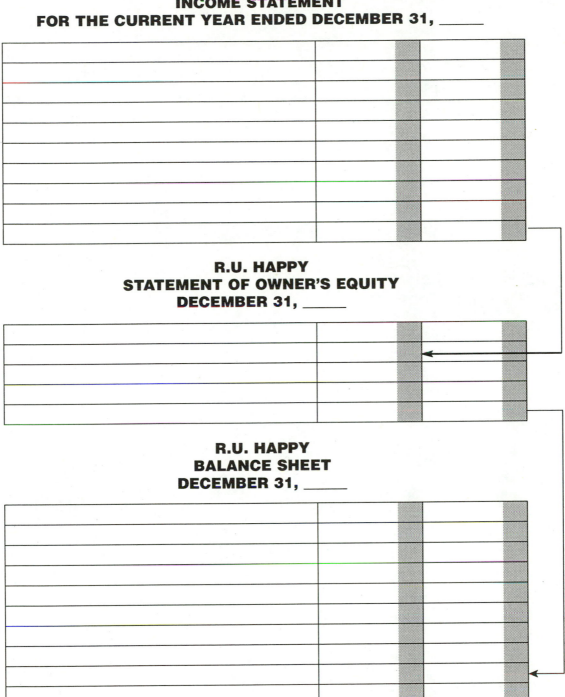

R.U. HAPPY
STATEMENT OF OWNER'S EQUITY
DECEMBER 31, _____

R.U. HAPPY
BALANCE SHEET
DECEMBER 31, _____

Basic Financial Statements

Ex. 7.   R.U. Happy started a business on January 1 with an investment of $13,000. During the year he withdrew $12,500 for personal use.

The balances of the business assets, liabilities, and owner's equity at the end of the year, December 31, are as follows:

CASH	$11,000
ACCOUNTS RECEIVABLE	3,100
SUPPLIES	2,100
ACCOUNTS PAYABLE	2,200
SERVICE INCOME	27,000
ADVERTISING EXPENSE	4,100
RENTAL EXPENSE	1,300
UTILITIES EXPENSE	400
SUPPLIES EXPENSE	6,000
MISCELLANEOUS EXPENSE	1,700

Instructions: Using the forms provided, prepare the following:

a)   An income statement for the current year.

b)   A statement of owner's equity at the end of the current year.

c)   A balance sheet as of December 31 of the current year.

(Continued)

R.U. HAPPY
INCOME STATEMENT
FOR THE CURRENT YEAR ENDED DECEMBER 31, _____

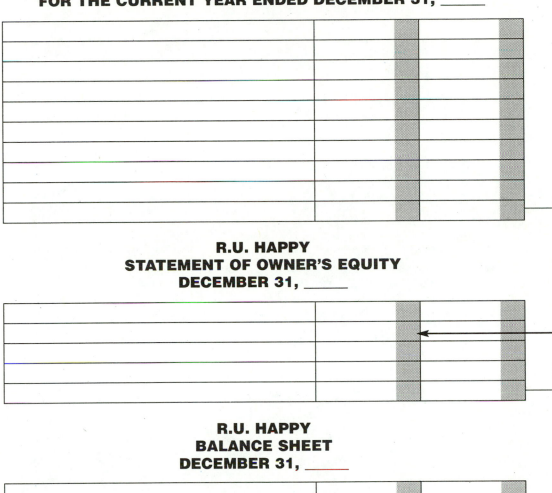

R.U. HAPPY
STATEMENT OF OWNER'S EQUITY
DECEMBER 31, _____

R.U. HAPPY
BALANCE SHEET
DECEMBER 31, _____

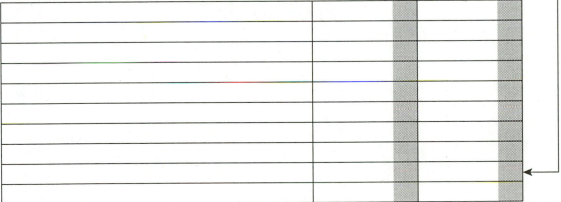

Mini-Problem: Journalizing, Posting, Trial Balance, and Financial Statements

Ex. 8.   Will U. Buyum began the Delicious Muffins Bakery on October 1 of the current year. During October, the following transactions were completed:

Oct.		
	1.	Invested cash, $10,000, and office equipment, $5,000.
	1.	Paid cash, $200, for baking supplies.
	2.	Bought baking equipment on account, $8,000.
	3.	Paid $500 for one month's business insurance policy.
	9.	Paid bakery help salaries of $1,000.
	16.	Paid $2,000 on account for amount owed from October 2.
	28.	Paid the month's utility bill, $700.
	30.	Withdrew $1,500 for personal use.
	31.	Bakery income for the month, all cash, totaled $6,000.
	31.	Determined that $175 of baking supplies had been used during the month.

Required:

a.   Using the following accounts, prepare general journal entries to record the above transactions: Cash; Baking Supplies; Office Equipment; Baking Equipment; Accounts Payable; Will U. Buyum, Capital; Will U. Buyum, Drawing; Bakery Income; Salary Expense; Baking Supplies Expense; Insurance Expense; and Utility Expense.

b.   Post the above transactions to the appropriate accounts in the general ledger updating balances when necessary.

c.   Prepare a trial balance.

d.   Prepare an income statement for the month of October.

e.   Prepare a statement of owner's equity as of October 31.

f.   Prepare a balance sheet dated October 31.

(Continued)

Journal   Page 1

Date	Description	P.R.	Debit	Credit

(Continued)

b)

GENERAL LEDGER

CASH   ACCOUNT NO. 11

Date	Item	P.R.	Debit	Credit	Balance	
					Debit	Credit

BAKING SUPPLIES   ACCOUNT NO. 12

Date	Item	P.R.	Debit	Credit	Balance	
					Debit	Credit

OFFICE EQUIPMENT   ACCOUNT NO. 13

Date	Item	P.R.	Debit	Credit	Balance	
					Debit	Credit

BAKING EQUIPMENT   ACCOUNT NO. 14

Date	Item	P.R.	Debit	Credit	Balance	
					Debit	Credit

(Continued)

ACCOUNTS PAYABLE   ACCOUNT NO. 21

Date	Item	P.R.	Debit	Credit	Balance	
					Debit	Credit

WILL U. BUYUM, CAPITAL   ACCOUNT NO. 31

Date	Item	P.R.	Debit	Credit	Balance	
					Debit	Credit

WILL U. BUYUM, DRAWING   ACCOUNT NO. 32

Date	Item	P.R.	Debit	Credit	Balance	
					Debit	Credit

BAKERY INCOME   ACCOUNT NO. 41

Date	Item	P.R.	Debit	Credit	Balance	
					Debit	Credit

SALARY EXPENSE   ACCOUNT NO. 51

Date	Item	P.R.	Debit	Credit	Balance	
					Debit	Credit

(Continued)

BAKING SUPPLIES EXPENSE   ACCOUNT NO. 52

Date	Item	P.R.	Debit	Credit	Balance	
					Debit	Credit

INSURANCE EXPENSE   ACCOUNT NO. 53

Date	Item	P.R.	Debit	Credit	Balance	
					Debit	Credit

UTILITIES EXPENSE   ACCOUNT NO. 54

Date	Item	P.R.	Debit	Credit	Balance	
					Debit	Credit

c) **Delicious Muffins Bakery**
TRIAL BALANCE
October 31, _____

d)

Delicious Muffins Bakery
INCOME STATEMENT
For Month Ended October 31, _____

(Continued)

e)

Delicious Muffins Bakery
STATEMENT OF OWNER'S EQUITY
October 31, _____

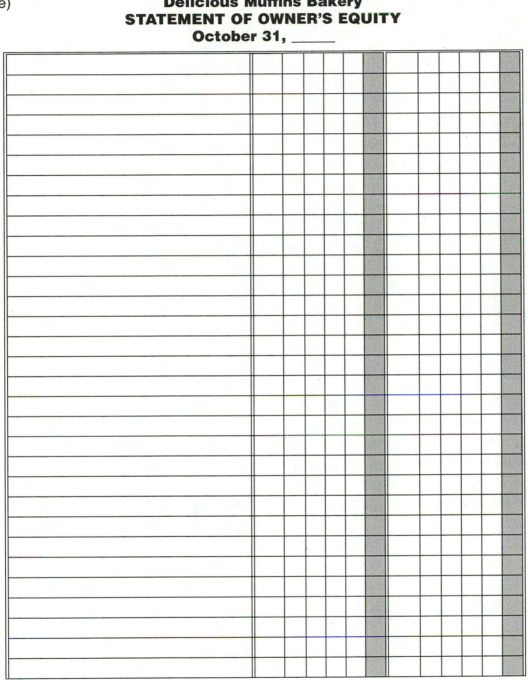

(Continued)

f)

Delicious Muffins Bakery
BALANCE SHEET
October 31, _____

NOTES

WORKPAPER FOR EXERCISES

EXERCISES

End of the Fiscal Period—Part One
Work Sheets and Adjusting Entries

Chapter Five

ACROSS

1 Cost minus accumulated depreciation
6 Made to bring up to date
8 Less than one year
10 Helping form; not required
11 Affecting the business itself
12 Account with an opposite balance
14 Reports net income or net loss

DOWN

2 Contains external and internal balances
3 Shows equation is in balance
4 Loss of value
5 What was paid for an asset
7 Outside the business
9 Asset that becomes expense when used
13 Longer than year or fiscal period

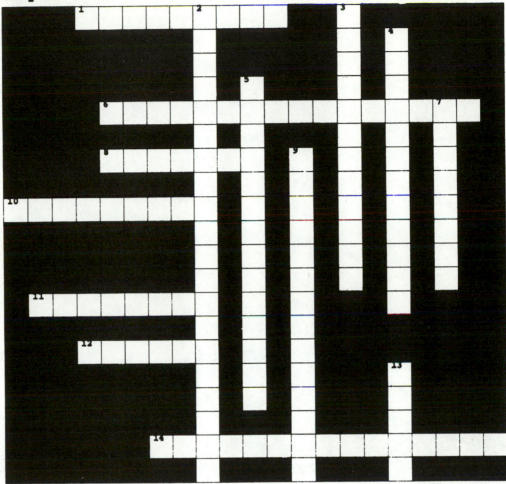

BOOK VALUE crossword puzzle:

Across:
- BOOK VALUE
- ADJUSTING ENTRIES
- CURRENT
- WORKSHEET
- INTERNAL
- CONTRA
- INCOME STATEMENT

Down:
- ADJUSTED TRIAL BALANCE
- HISTORICAL COST
- PREPAID EXPENSE
- BALANCE SHEET
- DEPRECIATION
- EXTERNAL
- FIXED

CHAPTER FIVE

END OF THE FISCAL PERIOD—Part One
Work Sheets and Adjusting Entries

EXERCISES

Extension of Accounts to Income Statement or Balance Sheet

Ex. 1. The following accounts are contained in the adjusted trial balance of Miles Delivery Service. Indicate whether the account would be extended to the income statement or balance sheet columns of a work sheet. Use the letters IS for income statement or BS for balance sheet. Also indicate whether the balance would be extended to the appropriate financial statement as a Dr. or a Cr. after selecting your choice of financial statement. The first account is presented as an example.

M. Away, Drawing	BS DR.	Accum. Depre. - Trucks	_____
Interest Earned	_____	Salary Expense	_____
Accounts Receivable	_____	Interest Receivable	_____
Rent Expense	_____	Deprec. Exp. - Trucks	_____
Accounts Payable	_____	Salaries Payable	_____
Cash	_____	Delivery Trucks	_____
Office Supplies	_____	M. Away, Capital	_____

The Two-Minute Warning

We are now at the end of the fiscal period. You have learned to analyze, journalize, post, prepare a trial balance, and prepare basic financial statements. What you have done would be what a business that had only external transactions would do. External transactions are those that affect our business and someone outside our business. Example—the buying of supplies on account.

Now let's find out how much money we made in a slightly different way! This new method requires the preparation of a **WORK SHEET**. A work sheet would be prepared by a business that has not only external transactions, but also internal transactions—those that affect only the business itself. Example—the using up of the supplies that we bought.

*Internal transactions are done on what is called a work sheet and are called "**adjustments**." Adjust means to "fix." These internal transactions need to be recorded at the end of a fiscal period in the "adjustments" column of your work sheet. The work sheet is not a financial statement, but rather a place for the accountant to gather information that will be needed to determine the net income (net loss) that the company had and to find the information needed to "close" the books.*

*As you will notice, each adjustment has both a **DR**. part and a **CR**. part. If these adjustments are not done, your company will not report the correct income (or loss).*

As you will also see, all adjustments in this chapter require a debit to an expense account—easy to remember! The balancing credit will go to what has been used up or what is owed.

Remember—all adjustments are made for the amounts *used* or *owed*!!!

NOW LET'S DO ONE!!!

Adjustments—What Account Would Be Debited/Credited?

Ex. 2. Identify the account that would be debited and the account that would be credited to record each of the following adjusting entries.

a. The amount of insurance that was used during the fiscal period.

b. The amount of salaries earned this fiscal period that will be paid next fiscal period.

c. Depreciation on the office equipment for the month.

d. The amount of supplies that had been used during the fiscal period.

Ex. 3. Complete the work sheet and record the necessary adjusting entries in the General Journal provided on the next page.

a) Ending Supplies Inventory, $200
b) Rent used for September, $750
c) Insurance used for September, $200
d) Depreciation for September on the Service Equipment, $500
e) Salaries owed for September, $300

MILES DELIVERY SERVICE
WORKSHEET
FOR THE MONTH ENDED SEPTEMBER 30, _____

Account Title	Trial Balance Debit	Trial Balance Credit	Adjustments Debit	Adjustments Credit	Adjusted Trial Balance Debit	Adjusted Trial Balance Credit	Income Statement Debit	Income Statement Credit	Balance Sheet Debit	Balance Sheet Credit
Cash	4085 –									
Accounts Receivable	1700 –									
Supplies	2200 –									
Prepaid Rent	2250 –									
Prepaid Insurance	1740 –									
Service Equipment	13500 –									
Accum. Depreciation										
Accounts Payable		1250 –								
Salaries Payable										
Miles Away, Capital		20650 –								
Miles Away, Drawing	1500 –									
Service Revenue		6400 –								
Salary Expense	1000 –									
Supplies Expense										
Rent Expense										
Depreciation Expense										
Insurance Expense										
Miscellaneous Expense	325 –									
TOTALS	28300 –	28300 –								

Journal   **Page**

Date	Description	P.R.	Debit	Credit

Ex. 4. Complete the work sheet and record the necessary adjusting entries in the General Journal provided on the next page.

a) Ending Supplies Inventory, $500
b) Rent used for September, $1125
c) Insurance used for September, $100
d) Depreciation for September on the Service Equipment, $100
e) Salaries owed for September, $200

MILES DELIVERY SERVICE
WORKSHEET
FOR THE MONTH ENDED SEPTEMBER 30, _____

Account Title	Trial Balance		Adjustments		Adjusted Trial Balance		Income Statement		Balance Sheet	
	Debit	Credit	Debit	Credit	Debit	Credit	Debit	Credit	Debit	Credit
Cash	4085 –									
Accounts Receivable	1700 –									
Supplies	2200 –									
Prepaid Rent	2250 –									
Prepaid Insurance	1740 –									
Service Equipment	13500 –									
Accum. Depreciation										
Accounts Payable		1250 –								
Salaries Payable										
Miles Away, Capital		20650 –								
Miles Away, Drawing	1500 –									
Service Revenue		6400 –								
Salary Expense	1000 –									
Supplies Expense										
Rent Expense										
Depreciation Expense										
Insurance Expense										
Miscellaneous Expense	325 –									
TOTALS	28300 –	28300 –								

Journal

Page

Date		Description	P.R.	Debit						Credit					

Ex. 5. Complete the work sheet and record the necessary adjusting entries in the General Journal provided on the next page.

a) Ending Supplies Inventory, $1500
b) Rent used for September, $500
c) Insurance used for September, $400
d) Depreciation for September on the Service Equipment, $200
e) Salaries owed for September, $600

MILES DELIVERY SERVICE
WORKSHEET
FOR THE MONTH ENDED SEPTEMBER 30, _____

Account Title	Trial Balance Debit	Trial Balance Credit	Adjustments Debit	Adjustments Credit	Adjusted Trial Balance Debit	Adjusted Trial Balance Credit	Income Statement Debit	Income Statement Credit	Balance Sheet Debit	Balance Sheet Credit
Cash	4085 –									
Accounts Receivable	1700 –									
Supplies	2200 –									
Prepaid Rent	2250 –									
Prepaid Insurance	1740 –									
Service Equipment	13500 –									
Accum. Depreciation										
Accounts Payable		1250 –								
Salaries Payable										
Miles Away, Capital		20650 –								
Miles Away, Drawing	1500 –									
Service Revenue		6400 –								
Salary Expense	1000 –									
Supplies Expense										
Rent Expense										
Depreciation Expense										
Insurance Expense										
Miscellaneous Expense	325 –									
TOTALS	28300 –	28300 –								

Journal   **Page**

Date	Description	P.R.	Debit	Credit

NOTES

WORKPAPER FOR EXERCISES

EXERCISES

CHAPTER 6

End of the Fiscal Period—Part Two
Closing Entries

ACROSS

4 Bringing balances to zero
5 Used one fiscal period
6 Closing entries bring capital to this
7 Number of closing entries

DOWN

1 Account used only during closing process
2 Account for all fiscal periods
3 Trial balance done end of fiscal period

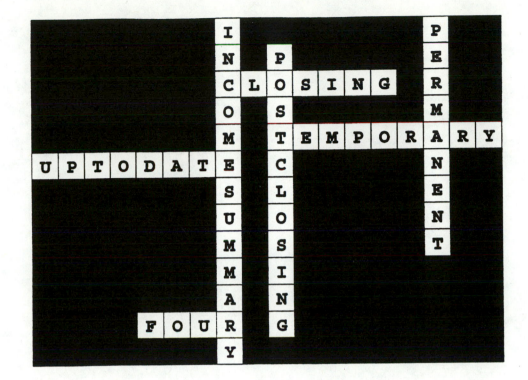

CHAPTER SIX

END OF THE FISCAL PERIOD—Part Two
Closing Entries

EXERCISES

Game Review—Closing the Books

Closing the books of a business is done at the end of a fiscal period. It means to get them ready for our next fiscal period. Many businesses close their books on December 31—but this is not a required date for this process.

In addition to preparing our accounts for the new fiscal period, closing the books also brings the balance of our capital account "up-to-date" so that it shows what we are worth at the end of the fiscal period rather than at the beginning of the fiscal period.

Closing the books takes 4 entries. They are called **"closing entries"** and are recorded in our journal, as are all entries.

Only **"temporary"** accounts are closed. As you remember, those are accounts whose balances are good for only the current fiscal period, i.e. revenues, expenses, and drawing.

Summary of the Closing Process

1. Done at the end of the fiscal period.

2. Brings the capital account up to date.

3. Brings the balances of the temporary accounts to zero.

4. Introduces a new "temporary" account called **Income Summary**.

5. Requires 4 journal entries.

When doing the following illustration of closing entries, think of your capital account as "mother", all the revenue, expense, and drawing accounts as her "children" and the new "temporary" account as the bus. The "bus," income summary, is used to "transport" the children home to "mother." This is what the first three closing entries are accomplishing. The fourth closing entry begins "drawing" home alone since drawing has no effect on income and is not allowed on the bus called "income summary."

Ex. 1

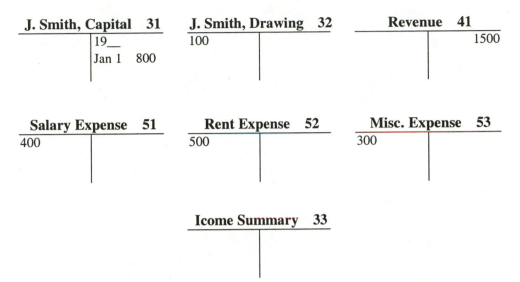

J. Smith, Capital 31	J. Smith, Drawing 32	Revenue 41
	19__		100				1500
	Jan 1 800				

Salary Expense 51	Rent Expense 52	Misc. Expense 53
400		500		300	

Icome Summary   33

Closing entries for January 31, _____:

1. Close Revenue into Income Summary.

2. Close Expenses into Income Summary.

3. Close the balance of Income Summary (net income) into Capital.

4. Close the balance of Drawing into Capital.

JOURNAL   Page

Date	Description	P.R.	Debit	Credit

Calculation of Net Income, Ending Capital, and Closing Entry Preparation

Ex. 2. The partially completed income statement columns below are from the work sheet of Miles Delivery Service.

   a. Calculate the amount of net income for the fiscal period.

   b. Assuming that in addition to the information provided below, Mr. Away withdrew $3,000 during the fiscal period, prepare the required closing entries.

   c. Assuming that Mr. Away had a capital balance of $45,000 at the beginning of the fiscal period, calculate his capital balance at the end of the fiscal period.

	Debit	**Credit**
Delivery Service Income		80,000
Salary Expense	36,000	
Insurance Expense	4,000	
Depreciation Expense, Trucks	10,000	
Supplies Expense	3,000	
Interest Expense	1,000	
Totals		_____
Net Income		======

Ex. 3. Record the closing entries required using the first work sheet that you completed in the previous chapter.

Sequence of Events During a Fiscal Period

Ex. 4. Arrange the following accounting "events" in proper sequence:

   a. Preparing financial statements.

   b. Preparing a post-closing trial balance.

   c. Journalizing daily transactions.

   d. Completing a work sheet.

   e. Journalizing and posting adjusting entries.

   f. Posting daily transactions.

   g. Preparing a trial balance.

   h. Journalizing and posting closing entries.

Ex. 2, part b.

Ex. 3

Date		Description	P.R.	Debit		Credit	

Journal   Page

Date	Description	P.R.	Debit	Credit

Ex. 5. Using the second work sheet that you completed for Miles Delivery Service in the previous chapter, record or prepare the following on the working papers provided:

a) Record the adjusting entries.

b) Record the closing entries.

c) Prepare an income statement.

d) Prepare a statement of owner's equity.

e) Prepare a balance sheet.

(Continued)

a) and b)

Journal   **Page**

Date	Description	P.R.	Debit	Credit

(Continued)

Journal

Page

Date		Description	P.R.	Debit						Credit					

(Continued)

c)

Miles Delivery Service
Income Statement
For Month Ended September 30, ____

(Continued)

d)

Miles Delivery Service
Statement of Owner's Equity
September 30, ____

(Continued)

e)

Miles Delivery Service
Balance Sheet
September 30, ____

ISDO™ SELF √ PRACTICE QUIZ 2

Work Sheets, Adjusting Entries, and Closing Entries

Answer the following questions either TRUE or FALSE:

1. A work sheet is a financial statement and is done after the income statement has been completed.

2. The adjusted trial balance is prepared before the trial balance.

3. The drawing account is the last account extended over to the income statement.

4. The amount brought to the balance sheet columns of the work sheet for the supplies account is larger than the amount on the trial balance.

5. After adjusting entries are entered into the work sheet, it is not necessary to record them in the general journal.

6. Adjusting entries, like all other entries, must be posted to the general ledger.

7. The only accounts that are closed are income statement accounts.

8. The account balances on a work sheet are extended from the adjusted trial balance to either the income statement or balance sheet columns.

Circle Your Choice:

1. The first set of columns on a work sheet are titled:

   A. balance sheet   B. income statement   C. trial balance   D. adjustments

2. The trial balance contains which of the following types of transactions:

   A. fraternal   B. internal   C. maternal   D. external

3. On a work sheet, the adjustment column contains amounts:

   A. used   B. not used   C. bought   D. charged

(Continued)

99

4. If the income statement columns and the balance sheet columns equal when they are first totaled, this would indicate:

    A. net loss   B. we must have   C. the company
                           added incorrectly   broke-even

5. A contra asset has the following type of balance:

    A. debit   B. credit   C. neither   D. both

6. The account accumulated depreciation contains the following in relation to a fixed asset:

    A. cost   B. value gained   C. value lost   D. future value

7. Which of the following would be part of the entry to close rent expense?

    A. debit to rent   B. credit to income   C. debit to   D. credit to
       expense   summary   capital   rent expense

NOTES

WORKPAPER FOR EXERCISES

EXERCISES

CHAPTER 7

Accounting for a
Merchandising Business

Chapter Seven

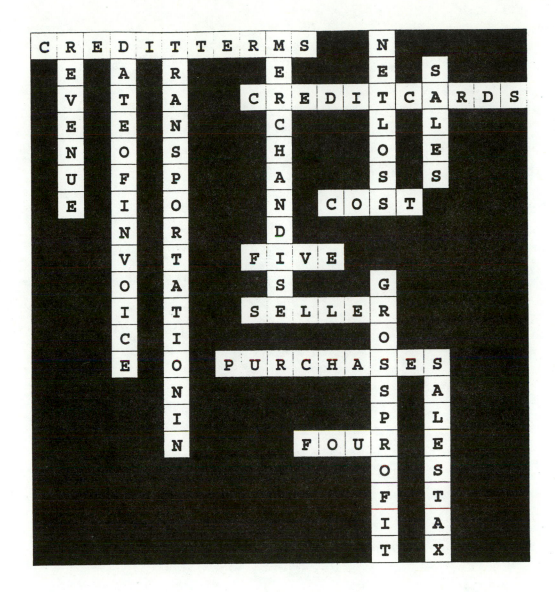

CHAPTER SEVEN

ACCOUNTING FOR A MERCHANDISING BUSINESS

EXERCISES

Do You Know Your Merchandising Accountanese?

Ex. 1. Place the letter for the appropriate term beside the statement that most closely defines it:

A.	Sales discount	F.	Merchandise
B.	Cash discount	G.	Gross profit
C.	Credit period	H.	FOB shipping point
D.	Purchase discount	I.	FOB destination
E.	Discount period.		

____1.   An agreement under which the buyer is responsible for the shipping charges.

____2.   A discount taken on goods bought or sold and paid or received within a stated period of time.

____3.   Goods that a company has bought and expects to sell to its customers.

____4.   A discount given when the amount owed for merchandise is received within the agreed upon period of time.

____5.   The time period agreed upon between the seller and the buyer for a reduction in price of merchandise.

____6.   An agreement under which the seller is responsible for the shipping charges.

____7.   The full time period that may pass before payment is due.

____8.   A discount taken when the amount owed for merchandise is paid within the agreed upon period of time.

____9.   The initial profit after deducting cost of goods sold from net sales.

Purchase of Merchandise Transactions

Ex. 2. Record general journal entries for the following transactions involving the buying of merchandise:

April   2. Purchased merchandise on account from Jones Company, $18,000. Shipping terms of FOB Shipping point. Credit terms of 1/10, N/30.

4. Paid the transportation charge on the purchase of April 2, $200.

6. Returned to Jones Company defective merchandise costing $3,000. Return transportation was the responsibility of the seller.

11. Paid Jones Company the balance due, net of the return and discount.

15. Recorded cash purchases of merchandise in the amount of $13,000.

Sales of Merchandise Transactions

Ex. 3. Record general journal entries for the following transactions involving the selling of merchandise.

April   2. Sold merchandise on account to Smith Company, $18,000. Shipping Terms of FOB shipping point. Credit terms of 1/10, N/30.

8. Merchandise previously sold to Smith Company on April 2 was returned, $3,000.

12. Received payment due from Smith Company from the sale of April 2, less the sale return and the sales discount.

Exercises 2 and 3

Journal

Page

Date	Description	P.R.	Debit	Credit

Purchase and Sale of Merchandise Transactions

Ex. 4. On June 5, Jackson Company purchased $21,000 of merchandise on account under the following terms: FOB shipping point, 2/15, N/30. Upon delivery of the merchandise, June 6, Jackson paid $200 to Star Transportation Services. After inspection of the merchandise it was determined that $1,000 was defective and returned to seller, Baker Company, on June 9. Baker Company received the merchandise back on June 10. On June 19, Jackson mailed a check for the amount due. Baker Company received the payment on June 20.

Required:

a. Record the general journal entries necessary for these events on the books of Jackson Company.

b. Record the general journal entries necessary for these events on the books of Baker Company.

Bank and NonBank Credit Card Sales Transactions

Ex. 5. Journalize the following transactions for bank credit card and nonbank credit card sales transactions. Use the general journal provided.

a. Sold merchandise to customers who used bank credit cards, $5,000.

b. Sold merchandise to customers who used nonbank credit cards, $6,000.

c. Mailed a check to the bank for processing fee on the bank credit card sales, $200.

d. Received a check for $5,640 from the nonbank credit card company for the money owed us from transaction b above. They had deducted a 6% service charge.

Net Sales and Gross Profit Calculations for a Merchandising Business

Ex. 6. Calculate the net sales and the gross profit for each of the following independent situations:

	a	b
Sales	$100,000	$85,000
Sales Returns and Allowances	15,000	9,000
Sales Discounts	2,000	1,000
Cost of Goods Sold	60,000	50,000

Exercises 4 and 5

Journal   **Page**

Date	Description	P.R.	Debit	Credit

Journal   Page

Date	Description	P.R.	Debit		Credit	

Cost of Good Sold Calculations

Ex. 7. During the current fiscal period Brownstone Company purchased merchandise costing $175,000. Determine their cost of goods sold under the following conditions:

    a.   They did not have a beginning or an ending inventory.

    b.   They had a beginning inventory of $40,000 but did not have an ending inventory.

    c.   They did not have a beginning inventory but did have an ending inventory of $20,000.

    d.   They had a beginning inventory of $43,000 and an ending inventory of $55,000.

Calculation of Amounts Using Basic Merchandising Business Formulas

Ex. 8. Using the following accounts and balances complete the requirements below:

	Debit	Credit
Beginning Inventory	$ 25,000	
Purchases	250,000	
Transportation–In	1,000	
Purchase Returns and Allowances		$ 20,000
Purchase Discount		5,000
Sales		450,000
Sales Returns and Allowances	18,000	
Sales Discounts	9,000	
Operating Expenses	140,000	

The ending inventory was $40,000

Required

    a.   Calculate the net sales.

    b.   Calculate the net purchases.

    c.   Calculate the cost of goods sold.

    d.   Calculate the gross profit.

    e.   Calculate the net income.

(Continued)

ISDO™ SELF √ PRACTICE QUIZ 3

Merchandising Business— Purchases and Sales

Indicate whether the following accounts are always debited or credited:

(Put an X in the correct column)

Account	Dr.	Cr.
Purchases		
Sales		
Transportation–In		
Sales Returns and Allowances		
Purchase Discount		
Purchase Returns and Allowances		
Sales Discounts		

Answer the following questions either **TRUE** or **FALSE.**

1. It is usual for the credit period in 2/10, N/30 to begin with the date that the merchandise was received.

2. Purchases of merchandise are debited to the purchases account when it is bought.

3. Discounts taken by the buyer for early payment of an invoice are called sales discounts by the buyer.

4. The effect of a sales return is to decrease revenue.

5. Under FOB shipping point, the seller is responsible for the transportation charges.

(Continued)

6. Under FOB destination, the seller is responsible for the transportation charges.

7. The account purchase returns and allowances always will be recorded as a credit.

8. Merchandise costing $1,500, terms 2/10, N/30, FOB shipping point, with transportation charges of $100 is bought. If the amount due is paid within the discount period, the discount allowed would be $32.

9. The account sales discount will always be recorded as a debit.

10. An entry for the transportation charges associated with buying and selling merchandise is always recorded on both the books of the buyer and the seller.

NOTES

WORKPAPER FOR EXERCISES

WORKPAPER FOR EXERCISES

WORKPAPER FOR EXERCISES

EXERCISES

CHAPTER **8**

Special Journals

Chapter Eight

ACROSS

2 Journal for anything bought on account
7 All journals are in this one
10 Indicates item is not posted

DOWN

1 Indicates posting of company name
3 Journal used for one type of transaction
4 Keeps records of companies and people
5 Journal used for all money coming in
6 Order of accounts in subsidiary ledger
7 Contains total amount owed to or owed by
8 Column used for all cash receipt entries
9 Posting at end of fiscal period

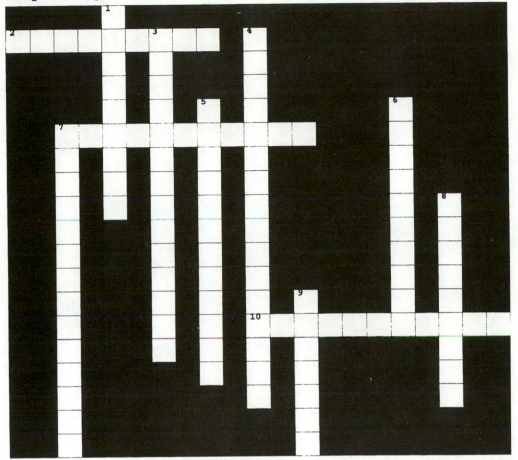

PURCHASES

COMBINATION

CHECK

SPECIAL JOURNAL

CASH RECEIPTS

SUBSIDIARY LEDGER

CONTROL ACCOUNT

CHECKMARK

ALPHABETIC

CASH DEBIT

DOUBLE CHECK

SUMMARY

CHAPTER EIGHT

SPECIAL JOURNALS

EXERCISES

Special Journal Identification

Ex. 1. Listed below are the five journals that were studied in this chapter. They have been given an abbreviation of one or two letters. Using those abbreviations, select the journal in which each transaction can be most appropriately recorded.

    CP Cash Payments   **P**   Purchase Journal

    CR Cash Receipts   **S**   Sales Journal

    G   General Journal

                                                             JOURNAL

a.   Recorded the cash sales for the week.   _____

b.   Paid the monthly rent.   _____

c.   Closed the drawing account.   _____

d.   Sold merchandise on account.   _____

e.   Sold merchandise for cash.   _____

f.   Adjusting entry for depreciation of building.   _____

g.   Purchased merchandise on account.   _____

h.   Owner invested additional cash into the business.   _____

(Continued)

i. Paid for supplies bought on account. _____

j. Paid cash to a customer for merchandise returned. _____

k. Paid amount owed for previous purchase of merchandise. _____

l. Issued credit for merchandise returned to us. _____

m. Received a check for amount owed to us. _____

n. Paid for insurance premium. _____

o. Borrowed money from a lending institution for 90 days. _____

p. Made a correcting entry. _____

q. Returned defective merchandise that had been bought on account. _____

r. Sold supplies on account at our cost. _____

s. Purchased merchandise for cash. _____

t. Returned defective merchandise that had been bought for cash. _____

Recording Sales Journal Transactions and Posting to Accounts Receivable Subsidiary Ledger

Ex. 2.   Special Journal

Sales Journal   Page 1

DATE		ACCOUNT DEBITED	P.R.	ACCT. RECEIVABLE DR. SALES CR.

ONE COLUMN USED FOR BOTH THE DEBIT AND THE CREDIT!!!

Transactions: Sold merchandise on account:

Dec.	1	Jones Co.	$300
	4	Smith Co.	$400
	8	Wills Co.	$500
	21	Jones Co.	$700
	27	Clay Co.	$100

General Ledger

Accounts Receivable 12

Control account. It tells us the total owed but does not tell who owes it to us or how much anyone owes!

Sales 41

Accounts Receivable Subsidiary Ledger

It contains the names of the companies that owe us money and shows how much is owed by each. Subsidiary ledgers (Manual System) are arranged in alphabetical order; not numerical.

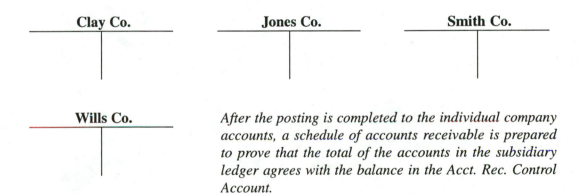

Clay Co.   **Jones Co.**   **Smith Co.**

Wills Co.

After the posting is completed to the individual company accounts, a schedule of accounts receivable is prepared to prove that the total of the accounts in the subsidiary ledger agrees with the balance in the Acct. Rec. Control Account.

Recording Cash Receipts Journal Transactions

Ex. 3.   Special Journal

Cash Receipts Journal   Page 1

DATE	ACCOUNT CREDITED	P.R.	GEN. CREDIT	SALES CREDIT	ACCTS. REC. CREDIT	SALES DIS. DEBIT	CASH DEBIT

a)   Record the following transactions in the cash receipts journal above:

June	1.	Received $400 from Jones Co. on account.
	3.	Received $470 from Smith Co. on account.
	5.	Received the balance owed from Clay Co., $600, less 2% discount.
	15.	Recorded cash sales from the 1st to the 15th in the amount of $4,000.
	21.	Received $1,000 from I.M. Rich, the owner, as an additional investment.
	28.	Received $800 cash from the sale of office supplies.

b)   Total, prove, and rule the Cash Receipts Journal.

Recording Purchase Journal Transactions

Ex. 4.   Special Journal

Purchases Journal   Page 1

DATE	ACCOUNT CREDITED	P.R.	ACCTS. PAY. CR.	PUR. DR.	STOR SUP. DR.	OFFICE SUP. DR.	OTHER ACCT. DEBIT		
							ACCT.	P.R.	AMT.

a)   Record the following transactions in the purchases journal above:

May   1.   Purchase merchandise on account from Williams Co., $5,000.

          2.   Purchased delivery equipment on account from Jones Delivery, $9,000.

          7.   Purchased merchandise on account from Davis Co., $3,000.

          10.   Purchased office supplies, $400, store supplies, $600, on account from Derby Supplies, Inc.

b)   Total, prove, and rule the Purchases Journal.

Recording Cash Payments Journal Transactions

Ex. 5.   Special Journal

Cash Payments Journal   Page 1

DATE	ACCOUNT DEBITED	P.R.	GENERAL DEBIT	ACCOUNTS PAYABLE DR.	PURCHASES DIS. CR.	CASH CREDIT

a)   Record the following transactions in the cash payments journal above:

May   1.   Paid the rent of $1,000.

4.   I.M. Rich, the owner, withdrew $200.

7.   Paid the amount owed, $5,000, to Baker Co. less 2% discount.

21.   Paid $300 to customer who returned merchandise we had previously sold to them.

28.   Paid monthly salaries of $7,000 as follows:
Office Salaries, $3,000
Administrative Salaries, $4,000.

b)   Total, prove, and rule the Cash Payments Journal.

Recording Miscellaneous Transactions in a General Journal

Ex. 6. Record the following transactions in the general journal provided below.

May   3.   Issued credit to a customer, Wilson Company, for damaged merchandise returned to us, $800.

            9.   Received credit for supplies that we did not want and returned to Clay Office Supply Store, $100.

          14.   Received credit for incorrect merchandise that we bought and returned to Shippen Company, $900.

Journal   Page 1

Date	Description	P.R.	Debit	Credit

Analysis of Transaction Through a Customers Account

Ex. 7. Debits and credits from three related transactions are shown below in the account of Willow Furniture Company, one of our accounts receivable. Describe what each transaction was and tell where each amount was posted from.

NAME   Willow Furniture Company
ADDRESS   47 South Willow Street
            Manchester, NH 03103

DATE		ITEM	P.R.	DEBIT	CREDIT	DR. BAL.
May	4		SJ40	7000 —		7000 —
	8		GJ9		1000 —	6000 —
	10		CR23		6000 —	—

Posting Reference Identification

Ex. 8. Based on the purchase journal illustrated below, identify each of the posting references, indicated by a number, as representing (a) a posting to a subsidiary ledger account, (b) a posting to a general ledger account, (c) that no posting is needed.

Purchases Journal   Page 1

DATE	ACCOUNT CREDITED	P.R.	ACCTS. PAY. CR.	PUR. DR.	STOR SUP. DR.	OFFICE SUP. DR.	OTHER ACCT. DEBIT		
							ACCT.	P.R.	AMT.
May 2	Jones Co.	(1)	500	500					
3	Smith Co.	(2)	600				Off. Eq.	(3)	600
11	Johnson Corp.	(4)	1000		600	400			
17	Williams Co.	(5)	2000	2000					
31	Totals		4100	2500	600	400			600
			(6)	(7)	(8)	(9)			(10)

Recording Transactions in All Special Journals and the General Journal

Ex. 9. The transactions given below were completed by Douglas Supply Store during the month of April.

Required

a. Record the transactions below in the journal that is most appropriate for each: sales journal, cash receipts journal, purchase journal, cash payments journal, or a general journal. Terms of all credit sales are 1/10, N30.

April	1.	Mr. Douglas invested $15,000 cash into the business.
	1.	Issued Check #1 for the April rent, $1,500.
	3.	Purchased store equipment on account from Sharp Equipment Company, $11,000. No discount.
	4.	Sold merchandise on account, Invoice #1, to Nixon Company, $3,000.

7. Purchased merchandise on account from Wellness Company, $8,000. Terms are 1/10, N/30.

9. Received check from Nixon Company for $2,970. This was for $3,000 that was owed less a 1% discount of $30.

10. Issued Check #2 for miscellaneous general expense, $300.

12. Received credit from Wellness Company for merchandise we returned to them, $1,000.

14. Sold merchandise on account, Invoice #2, to Collins Company, $6,000.

15. Issued check #3 for $11,000 to Sharp Equipment Company in payment of amount owed.

15. Recorded the cash sales for April 1–15, $25,000.

16. Issued check #4 for balance due to Wellness Company, $6,930. This was after deducting the amount previously returned and a discount of 1%; $70.

17. Issued credit to Collins Company, $2,000, for merchandise returned to us from sale of April 14.

17. Received check from Stapleton Company for amount owed, no discount, $2,000.

18. Purchased merchandise on account, $4,000, from Wallace Company. Terms 2/10, N/30.

19. Purchased merchandise on account, $9,000, from Larson Company. No discount. Terms are Net 10 days.

23. Issued check #5 to Union Leader Corporation for advertising, $500.

24. Received check for $3,960 representing balance due from Collins Company; $6,000 original sales less $2,000 return and discount of 1%.

25. Sold merchandise on account, Invoice #3, $18,000 to Pierson Company.

26. Purchased store supplies, $300 and office supplies, $200 on account from Staplemax Supply Company. No discount.

27. Issued credit to Pierson Company for return of $3,000 of merchandise sold on the 25th.

28. Paid the $9,000 owed to Larson Company, no discount. Check #6.   (Continued)

29. Mr. Douglas made a personal withdrawal of $2,000. Check #7.

30. Paid monthly salaries of $9,000 as follows: sales salaries, $6,000; office salaries, $3,000. Issued check #8.

30. Recorded the cash sales for April 16–30, $28,000.

b. Total, prove, and rule each of the special journals.

Sales Journal   Page 1

DATE	INV. NO.	ACCOUNT DEBITED	P.R.	ACCT. RECEIVABLE DR. SALES CR.

Cash Receipts Journal   Page 1

DATE	ACCOUNT CREDITED	P.R.	GENERAL CREDIT	SALES CREDIT	ACCTS. REC. CREDIT	SALES DISCOUNT DEBIT	CASH DEBIT

(Continued)

Purchases Journal   Page 1

DATE	ACCOUNT CREDITED	P.R.	ACCTS. PAY. CR.	PUR. DR.	STOR SUP. DR.	OFFICE SUP. DR.	OTHER ACCTS. DR.		
							TITLE	P.R.	AMT.

Cash Payments Journal   Page 1

DATE	CHK. NO.	ACCOUNT DEBITED	P.R.	GENERAL DEBIT	ACCOUNTS PAYABLE DR.	PURCHASE DISCOUNT CREDIT	CASH CREDIT

(Continued)

Journal   **Page**

Date	Description	P.R.	Debit	Credit

Recording Transactions in All Special Journals and the General Journal

Ex. 10. The following transactions were completed by Stedman Furniture Store during May of the current year.

Required

a. Record the transactions in the journal that is most appropriate for each: sales journal, cash receipts journal, purchase journal, cash payments journal, or a general journal. **Terms of all sales on account are 1/10, N/30. Terms of all purchases of merchandise are 2/10, N/30. Begin numbering checks with 101. Begin numbering sales invoices with 51.**

May	1.	Lois Stedman invested $45,000 cash into her business.
	2.	Issued check for May rent, $2,000.
	3.	Bought store equipment on account from Kline Equipment, $20,000. No discount. Net 30 days.
	4.	Issued invoice to Baker Company, $11,000 for merchandise sold on account.
	5.	Purchased merchandise on account from Crane Company, $17,000.
	6.	Received check from Nicholson Company for $9,900. This was in payment of amount owed from previous sale less $100 discount.
	7.	Issued check for postage expense, $45.
	7.	Issued credit to Baker Company for $1,000. This was a return of merchandise sold to them on May 4.
	10.	Received balance due, after return and discount, from Baker Company, from transactions of May 4 and May 7.
	11.	Issued invoice to Lamar Company, $18,000, for merchandise sold on account.

(Continued)

12. Issued check to Globe Advertising for advertisement in magazine, $300.

14. Issued check for amount owed to Crane Company, less discount, for purchase on the 5th.

15. Recorded cash sales for May 1–15, $50,000.

16. Purchased office supplies, $500, and store supplies, $700, on account from Supermax Supply Company. No discount.

18. Issued check for cash purchase of merchandise, $12,000.

19. Received credit from Supermax Supply Company for $100 of store supplies returned to them.

20. Purchased merchandise on account from Belisle Brothers, $13,000.

21. Received a check for the balance due, less discount, from Lamar Company for sale on the 11th.

22. Received a check for $2,000 for damaged merchandise bought on the 18th that we returned.

24. Issued check, $400, for miscellaneous general expense.

25. Received credit from Belisle Brothers, $2,000, for the merchandise we returned to them from the 20th.

27. Issued check to Kline Company on account, $20,000, for the store equipment bought on the 3rd.

30. Issued check to Belisle Brothers for balance due, less return and discount, from purchase on the 20th.

30. Issued check for monthly salaries, $15,000; sales salaries, $8,000; office salaries, $7,000.

31. Recorded cash sales from May 16–31, $48,000.

31. Received a check, $50, from the sale of office supplies to another business in the building as an accommodation.

b. Total, prove, and rule each of the special journals.

(Continued)

Sales Journal   Page 1

DATE	INV. NO.	ACCOUNT DEBITED	P.R.	ACCT. RECEIVABLE DR. SALES CR.	

Cash Receipts Journal   Page 1

DATE	ACCOUNT CREDITED	P.R.	GEN. CREDIT	SALES CREDIT	ACCTS. REC. CREDIT	SALES DIS. DEBIT	CASH DEBIT

(Continued)

Purchases Journal   Page 1

DATE	ACCOUNT CREDITED	P.R.	ACCTS. PAY. CR.	PUR. DR.	STOR SUP. DR.	OFFICE SUP. DR.	OTHER ACCTS. DR.		
							TITLE	P.R.	AMT.

Cash Payments Journal   Page 1

DATE	CHK. NO.	ACCOUNT DEBITED	P.R.	GENERAL DEBIT	ACCOUNTS PAYABLE DR.	PURCHASE DISCOUNT CREDIT	CASH CREDIT

(Continued)

Journal   Page

Date	Description	P.R.	Debit	Credit

NOTES

WORKPAPER FOR EXERCISES

Journal   **Page**

Date	Description	P.R.	Debit	Credit

EXERCISES

CHAPTER 9

**Merchandising Business
End of the Fiscal Period**

Chapter Nine

ACROSS

4 Simplest income statement

7 Entries that bring up-to-date

8 Inventory type always being up-dated

DOWN

1 On hand last day of fiscal period

2 Detailed financial statements

3 Owned for resale

5 Actual count of inventory

6 Revenue minus contra revenue

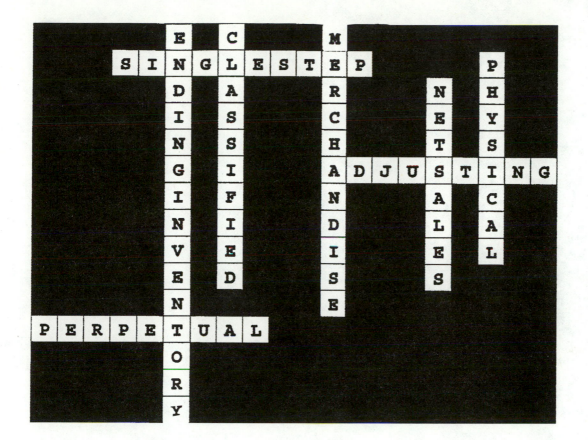

CHAPTER NINE

MERCHANDISING BUSINESS
End of the Fiscal Period

EXERCISES

Ending Merchandise Inventory Adjusting Entry

Ex. 1. The following information was obtained from the records of Crandall Company at the end of the current fiscal period:

Merchandise inventory at the beginning of the fiscal period $150,000

Merchandise inventory at the end of the fiscal period $147,000

Required

a. Record the necessary transaction to reflect the decrease in the inventory at the end of the fiscal period.

General Journal   Page 1

DATE	DESCRIPTION	P.R.	DEBIT	CREDIT

b. Does the transaction required in letter a indicate that $3,000 of merchandise must have been stolen during the fiscal period? If not, what caused the reduction in the beginning inventory?

Ex. 2. Complete the following work sheet, and record the necessary adjusting and closing entries in the General Journal provided on the next page.

a) Ending Merchandise Inventory, $83,000
b) Ending Supplies Inventory $150
c) Rent used for December, $3,000
d) Depreciation for December on the Store Equipment, $3,500
e) Salaries owed for December, $3,000

JOHNSON FRAMING SHOP
WORK SHEET
FOR MONTH ENDED DECEMBER 31, _____

Account Title	Trial Balance Debit	Trial Balance Credit	Adjustments Debit	Adjustments Credit	Adjusted Trial Balance Debit	Adjusted Trial Balance Credit	Income Statement Debit	Income Statement Credit	Balance Sheet Debit	Balance Sheet Credit
Cash	20900 –									
Accounts Receivable	25700 –									
Merchandise Inventory	83400 –									
Office Supplies	2150 –									
Prepaid Rent	18000 –									
Store Equipment	42000 –									
Accumulated Depreciation		11500 –								
Accounts Payable		19350 –								
Salaries Payable										
Ted Johnson, Capital		120900 –								
Ted Johnson, Drawing	4000 –									
Income Summary										
Sales		158290 –								
Sales Returns/Allowances	2200 –									
Sales Discounts	3180 –									
Purchases	88160 –									
Purchase Returns/Allowances		2050 –								
Purchase Discount		1850 –								
Transportation - In	9600 –									
Advertising Expense	1900 –									
Depreciation Expense										
Office Supplies Expense										
Rent Expense										
Salary Expense	12000 –									
Utilities Expense	750 –									
TOTALS	313940 –	313940 –								

Journal

Date		Description	P.R.	Debit						Credit					

Journal

Date	Description	P.R.	Debit	Credit

Ex. 3. Complete the following work sheet, and record the necessary adjusting and closing entries in the General Journal provided on the next page.

a) Ending Merchandise Inventory, $84,400
b) Ending Supplies Inventory $650
c) Rent used for December, $2,000

d) Depreciation for December on the Store Equipment, $1,500
e) Salaries owed for December, $500

JOHNSON FRAMING SHOP
WORK SHEET
FOR MONTH ENDED DECEMBER 31, _____

Account Title	Trial Balance Debit	Trial Balance Credit	Adjustments Debit	Adjustments Credit	Adjusted Trial Balance Debit	Adjusted Trial Balance Credit	Income Statement Debit	Income Statement Credit	Balance Sheet Debit	Balance Sheet Credit
Cash	20900 –									
Accounts Receivable	25700 –									
Merchandise Inventory	83400 –									
Office Supplies	2150 –									
Prepaid Rent	18000 –									
Store Equipment	42000 –									
Accumulated Depreciation		11500 –								
Accounts Payable		19350 –								
Salaries Payable										
Ted Johnson, Capital		120900 –								
Ted Johnson, Drawing	4000 –									
Income Summary										
Sales		158290 –								
Sales Returns/Allowances	2200 –									
Sales Discounts	3180 –									
Purchases	88160 –									
Purchase Returns/Allowances		2050 –								
Purchase Discount		1850 –								
Transportation - In	9600 –									
Advertising Expense	1900 –									
Depreciation Expense										
Office Supplies Expense										
Rent Expense										
Salary Expense	12000 –									
Utilities Expense	750 –									
TOTALS	313940 –	313940 –								

Journal   Page 1

Date		Description	P.R.	Debit						Credit					

Journal   Page 2

Date	Description	P.R.	Debit	Credit

Ex. 4.   Complete the following work sheet, and record the necessary adjusting and closing entries in the General Journal provided on the next page.

a) Ending Merchandise Inventory, $86,000
b) Ending Supplies Inventory $300
c) Rent used for December, $3,000
d) Depreciation for December on the Store Equipment, $5,000
e) Salaries owed for December, $700

JOHNSON FRAMING SHOP
WORK SHEET
FOR MONTH ENDED DECEMBER 31, _____

Account Title	Trial Balance Debit	Trial Balance Credit	Adjustments Debit	Adjustments Credit	Adjusted Trial Balance Debit	Adjusted Trial Balance Credit	Income Statement Debit	Income Statement Credit	Balance Sheet Debit	Balance Sheet Credit
Cash	20900 –									
Accounts Receivable	25700 –									
Merchandise Inventory	83400 –									
Office Supplies	2150 –									
Prepaid Rent	18000 –									
Store Equipment	42000 –									
Accumulated Depreciation		11500 –								
Accounts Payable		19350 –								
Salaries Payable										
Ted Johnson, Capital		120900 –								
Ted Johnson, Drawing	4000 –									
Income Summary										
Sales		158290 –								
Sales Returns/Allowances	2200 –									
Sales Discounts	3180 –									
Purchases	88160 –									
Purchase Returns/Allowances		2050 –								
Purchase Discount		1850 –								
Transportation - In	9600 –									
Advertising Expense	1900 –									
Depreciation Expense										
Office Supplies Expense										
Rent Expense										
Salary Expense	12000 –									
Utilities Expense	750 –									
TOTALS	313940 –	313940 –								

Journal

Page 1

Date	Description	P.R.	Debit	Credit

Journal

Date	Description	P.R.	Debit	Credit

Mini-Problem for a Merchandising Business at the End of the Fiscal Period

Ex. 5.   The following accounts are from the adjusted trial balance of the Smith Company work sheet at the end of the current fiscal year, December 31.

	Debit	Credit
Cash	$60,000	
Merchandise Inventory	35,000	
Accounts Receivable	35,000	
Supplies	3,000	
Prepaid Insurance	7,000	
Store Equipment	47,000	
Accumulated Depreciation–Store Equipment		$ 10,000
Accounts Payable		20,000
Interest Payable		2,000
Note Payable (3 year, $5,000 due next year)		15,000
Lee Smith, Capital		118,000
Lee Smith, Drawing	15,000	
Income Summary		2,000
Sales		225,000
Sales Returns and Allowances	17,000	
Sales Discounts	2,000	
Purchases	95,000	
Transportation–In	3,000	
Purchase Returns and Allowances		5,000
Purchase Discounts		1,700
Sales Salaries Expense	30,000	
Rent Expense (Selling)	8,000	
Store Supplies Expense	4,000	
Advertising Expense	16,000	
Office Salaries Expense	18,000	
Rent Expense (Office)	2,000	
Office Supplies Expense	1,700	
Totals	$398,700	$398,700

A physical inventory had determined that there was $33,000 of merchandise on hand at the beginning of the fiscal period.

(Continued)

Required

a. Calculate the net sales for the year.

b. Calculate the cost of merchandise available to be sold.

c. Calculate the cost of goods sold.

d. Calculate the gross profit.

e. Is it possible that the gross profit could become a net loss? If so, what would cause this?

f. Using the account titles and balances given above, prepare a classified income statement in acceptable format.

g. Using the account titles and balances given above, prepare a single-step income statement in acceptable format.

h. Prepare a statement of owner's equity for December 31. Assume that no additional investments were made during the month.

i. Prepare a classified balance sheet using the above account titles, balances, and previously prepared financial statements when necessary.

(Continued)

f)

Smith Company
Income Statement
For Year Ended December 31, _____

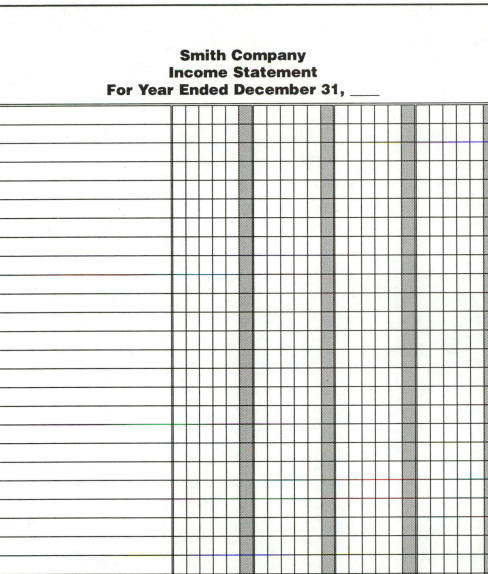

(Continued)

g)

Smith Company
Income Statement
For Year Ended December 31, ____

(Continued)

h)

Smith Company
Statement of Owner's Equity
December 31, ____

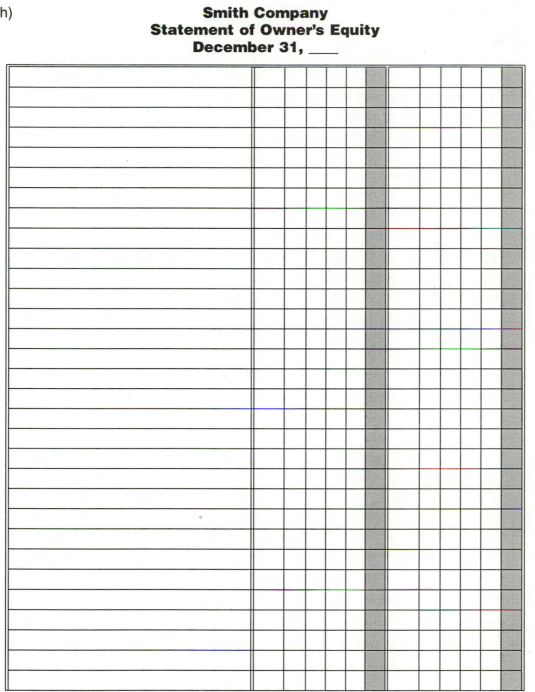

(Continued)

i)

Smith Company
Balance Sheet
December 31, ____

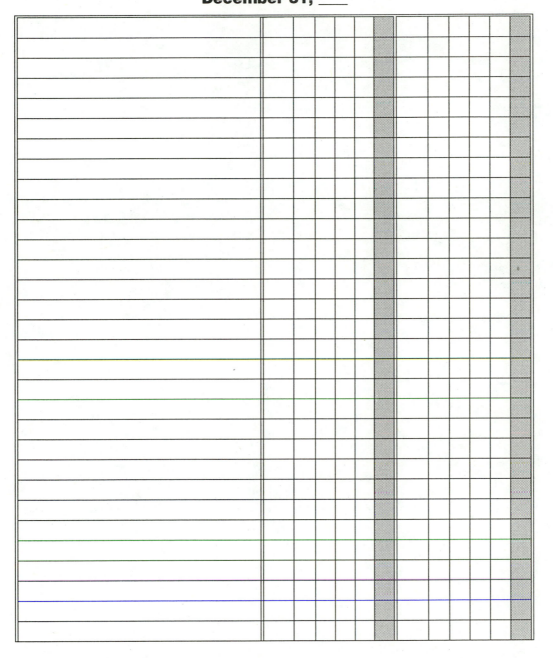

(Continued)

NOTES

WORKPAPER FOR EXERCISES

EXERCISES

CHAPTER 10

Internal Control
Control of Cash

Chapter Ten

ACROSS

1 Used to balance petty cash
6 Used for small payments of cash
8 Protect the assets of a business
9 Brings checkbook and bank into agreement

DOWN

1 Charged by bank
2 Bring petty cash to where it was
3 Checks not cleared
4 Filled out for petty cash use
5 Set up petty cash fund
7 Not enough money to cover check

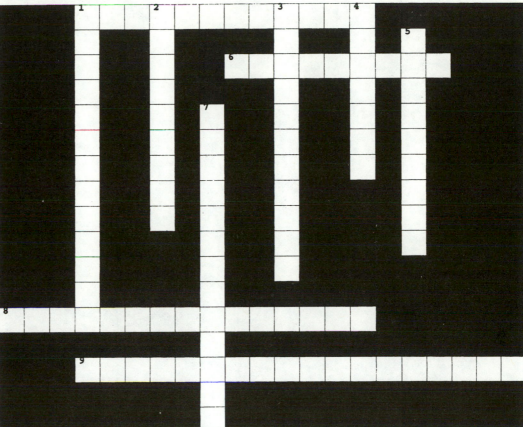

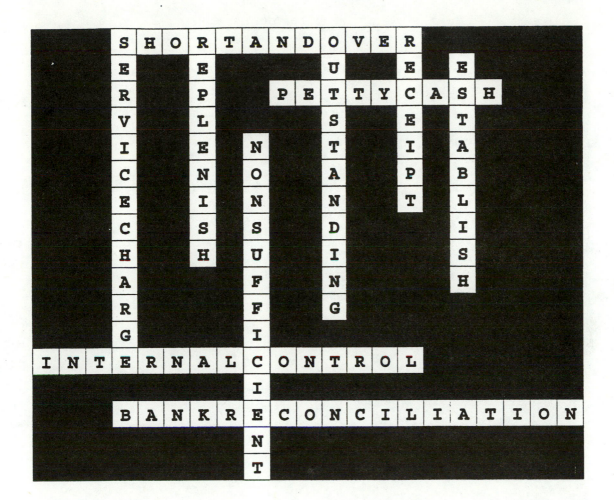

CHAPTER TEN

INTERNAL CONTROL
Control of Cash

EXERCISES

Internal Control

Ex. 1. Friends Company recently hired their first bookkeeper. The bookkeeper is nowhere to be found and about $75,000 is missing. The company hired auditors who discovered that the bookkeeper had written and signed several checks made out to a friend. The bookkeeper had entered these payments as part of the company's salary expense. The friend, who had never worked for the company, cashed the checks and, you guessed it, ran away with the bookkeeper. The company later discovered that it did not have insurance for this loss.

How could this type of loss have been prevented?

NOTE:

ENTRIES REQUIRED IN THE FOLLOWING EXERCISES ALL INVOLVE THE RECEIPT OR PAYMENT OF CASH. THEY SHOULD BE RECORDED IN EITHER A CASH RECEIPTS OR A CASH PAYMENTS JOURNAL. HOWEVER, IN ORDER TO EMPHASIZE AND REINFORCE THE ACCOUNTS NEEDED FOR THESE ENTRIES, WE WILL BE RECORDING THEM IN GENERAL JOURNAL FORM.

Collections by the bank

Ex. 2. A bank statement indicated that the bank had collected an interest-bearing note for Clausen Company in the amount of $5,750; $750 of which was interest. Record the entry required on the books of Clausen Company to record this event.

(Continued)

General Journal   Page 7

Date	Description	P.R.	Debit	Credit

Cash short and over

Ex. 3.   The cash register tape indicated there should have been $6,152 in the cash register drawer. The actual cash counted was $6,150. Record the entry to record the receipt of cash from the cash sales for the day.

General Journal   Page 9

Date	Description	P.R.	Debit	Credit

Petty Cash, establishment and replenishment

Ex. 4. a. Record the entry necessary to establish a petty cash fund for $60.

b. Record the entry necessary to replenish the petty cash fund as follows:

Film rental	$12
Refreshments	30
Postage	5
Printing	8

There is $5 remaining in the petty cash box at the time of replenishment.

General Journal   Page 3

Date	Description	P.R.	Debit	Credit

Petty Cash, establishment, replenishment, and increasing

Ex. 5. a. Record the entry necessary to establish a petty cash fund for $400.

b. Record the entry necessary to replenish the petty cash fund as follows:

Postage	$ 85
Transportation	10
Store supplies	90
Miscellaneous	150

There is $65 remaining in the petty cash box at the time of replenishment.

c. Record the entry necessary to increase the petty cash account up to $500.

General Journal   Page 4

Date	Description	P.R.	Debit	Credit

Ex. 6.   Assume that in Exercise 5 above, that instead of $65 being in the petty cash box prior to replenishment, there was only $61. Record the required entry for this situation.

General Journal   Page 6

Date	Description	P.R.	Debit	Credit

Bank reconciliation adjustments

Ex. 7.   a.   Indicate whether the following affect the bank balance side or your checkbook side when completing a bank reconciliation.

   a. Interest earned
   b. Bank service charges
   c. Outstanding checks
   d. NSF checks
   e. Outstanding deposits
   f. Amounts collected for us by the bank

   b.   Which of the above would require entries in our accounting records?

General Journal

Bank reconciliation and entries

Ex. 8.   The balance in the checkbook of Flynn Company is $20,100. Upon receiving their monthly bank statement, there seems to be a discrepancy. They show we have $20,000. Before calling the bank you decide to do a bank reconciliation. You find the following information:

a.   There are outstanding checks of $5,000.

b.   A deposit that we made for $5,100 does not appear on the bank statement.

c.   The bank had collected a non-interest bearing note on our behalf for $700.

d.   The bank had charged our account $750 for a check written correctly for $75.

e.   The bank had charged us a service charge of $34.

f.   We had written a check correctly for $56 but had entered it in our records as $65. The check was for payment of an amount owed.

Required

1.   Prepare a bank reconciliation from the information above.

BANK STATEMENT BALANCE   CHECKBOOK BALANCE

(Continued)

2. Prepare general journal entries required as a result of the bank reconciliation.

General Journal   Page 2

Date	Description	P.R.	Debit	Credit

Bank reconciliation and entries

Ex. 9. The balance in the checkbook of the Weld Corporation indicates a balance of $45,300. The bank statement, just received, shows a balance of $45,800. In gathering information for the bank reconciliation you find:

a. Outstanding checks for $7,550.

b. Outstanding deposits of $?????

c. Bank service charges of $75.

d. The bank had collected an interest-bearing note for us in the amount of $6,300. This amount included the face of the note receivable and $300 interest.

e. The bank had charged a check against our account for $900. The correct amount should have been $990.

f. We had written a check correctly for $780. Our checkbook indicates the

(Continued)

check, written for an amount owed, was entered on our books as $870.

Required

1. Determine what the total of the outstanding deposits must have been in order for the bank reconciliation to balance.

   BANK STATEMENT   CHECKBOOK BALANCE

2. Record the entries required on the books of the Weld Corporation as a result of this bank reconciliation.

General Journal   Page 2

Date		Description	P.R.	Debit		Credit	

NOTES

WORKPAPER FOR EXERCISES

WORKPAPER FOR EXERCISES

Journal   **Page**

Date	Description	P.R.	Debit	Credit

Journal   Page

Date	Description	P.R.	Debit	Credit

EXERCISES

CHAPTER 11

Statement of Cash Flows
An Introduction

Cashflow

ACROSS

2 Least used statement method.
4 Day to day business activities.
5 Statements of this year and last year.

DOWN

1 From external activities.
3 Support running of company.
5 Statement of source and use of cash.
6 Record when earned or incurred.
7 Number one statement method.

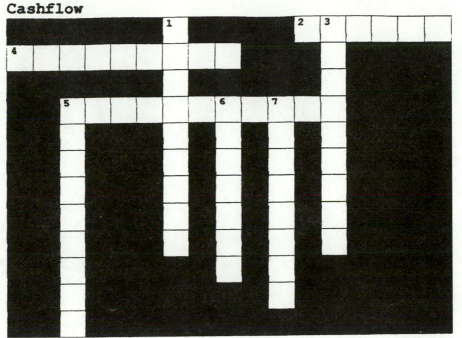

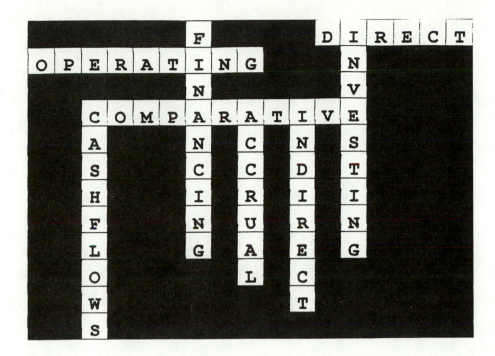

CHAPTER ELEVEN

STATEMENT OF CASH FLOWS
An Introduction

EXERCISES

Ex. 1. Using the choices given below, a through g, select the word that best describes the definitions below.

a. Comparative financial statements
b. Depreciation expense
c. Direct method
d. Financing activities

e. Indirect method
f. Investing activities
g. Operating activities

_____1. Activities of a company that are related to fixed assets.

_____2. An occurrence that reduces net operating income, but that does not require cash.

_____3. Reconciles the cash provided from business activities to net income from the accrual basis of accounting.

_____4. Accounting reports that provide information for two or more consecutive fiscal periods.

_____5. Activities of a company that involve the creation of debt or equity and the payment of dividends.

_____6. Activities of a company that are related to the everyday activities of a company.

_____7. Presents specific details of the individual cash inflow and cash outflow of a business.

Ex. 2. Place the letter "I" next to any of the following items that are considered to be inflows of cash to a company. Place the letter "O" next to any of the following items that are considered to be outflows of cash by a business.

_____ 1. Prepaid insurance decreased.

_____ 2. Merchandise inventory increased.

_____ 3. Accounts payable decreased.

_____ 4. Fixed assets increased.

_____ 5. Taxes payable decreased.

_____ 6. Common stock increased.

_____ 7. Salaries payable increased.

_____ 8. Accounts receivable decreased.

_____ 9. Notes payable increased.

_____10. Dividend obligation fulfilled.

Ex. 3. Classify the following as one of the three business activities associated with a statement of cash flows.

> a. operating activities
> b. investing activities
> c. financing activities

_____ 1. Buying equipment.

_____ 2. Paying dividends.

_____ 3. Borrowing from other companies.

_____ 4. Adjusting net income for depreciation expense.

_____ 5. Buying additional supplies.

_____ 6. Issuing common and preferred stock.

_____ 7. Payment of tax obligations.

_____ 8. Involve changes in current assets or current liabilities.

_____ 9. Involve changes in fixed assets.

_____10. Involve changes in fixed liabilities or stockholder's equity.

Ex. 4. Using the information provided below, prepare the operating activities section for the Miles Delivery Service statement of cash flows. Assume the net income for the current fiscal period was $3,000. Also assume depreciation expense of the current fiscal period was $200.

An analysis of the comparative balance sheets for last year and the current year revealed the following changes:

Current Assets:

Accounts Receivable	Decrease of $400
Merchandise Inventory	Increase of $300
Supplies	Decrease of $25

Current Liabilities:

Accounts Payable	Increase of $600
Notes Payable	Decrease of $175

Ex. 5. The following needed information was obtained from the accounting records of Miles Delivery Company at the end of the current year. Use this information to prepare a Statement of Cash Flows to show how cash increased by $4,000 during the current fiscal period. Dividends paid during the year amounted to $200.

From the current years income statement:

Net Income	$12,000
Depreciation Expense	1,000

From the comparative balance sheets of this year and last year:

Current Assets:		
Accounts Receivable	Decrease	$300
Mdse. Inventory	Increase	100
Prepaid Rent	Increase	600
Fixed Assets:		
Buildings	Increase	$9,000
Accum. Depre.–Bld.	Increase	1,000
Current Liabilities:		
Accounts Payable	Decrease	$900
Fixed Liabilities:		
3 year Note Payable	Increase	$800
Stockholder's Equity:		
Common Stock	Increase	$700

Ex. 6. The following needed information was obtained from the accounting records of Miles Delivery Company at the end of the current year. Use this information to prepare a Statement of Cash Flows to show how cash increased by $28,700 during the current fiscal period. Dividends paid during the year amounted to $4,000.

From the current years income statement:

Net Income	$35,000
Depreciation Expense	5,000

From the comparative balance sheets of this year and last year:

Current Assets:

Accounts Receivable	Increase	$6,000
Mdse. Inventory	Increase	3,000
Prepaid Insurance	Decrease	700

Fixed Assets:

Buildings	Increase	$15,000
Accum. Depre.–Bld.	Increase	5,000
Investment in X Company	Decrease	8,000

Current Liabilities:

Accounts Payable	Increase	$6,000
Notes Payable	Decrease	1,000

Fixed Liabilities:

Bonds Payable	Increase	$8,000

Stockholder's Equity:

Common Stock	Decrease	$5,000

Answer the following questions after your preparation of the Statement of Cash Flows:

a. For which type of business activity did Miles use most of their cash?

b. From which type of business activity did Miles obtain most of their cash?

c. Over the long term of business operations, are these appropriate sources and uses of cash?

WORKPAPER FOR EXERCISES

WORKPAPER FOR EXERCISES

WORKPAPER FOR EXERCISES

EXERCISES

CHAPTER 12

Financial Statement Analysis
An Introduction

ACROSS

4 Alternate name of owner's equity.
6 Less than one year.
10 Relationship between two numbers
12 How effective assets are being used.

DOWN

1 Ease of becoming cash.
2 Greater than one year.
3 Comparison of results.
5 Worth of stock in company records.
7 Amount each share of common stock made.
8 Ease of producing income.
9 Ability to meet long-term debt.
11 Represented by owners of the business.

Statement Analysis

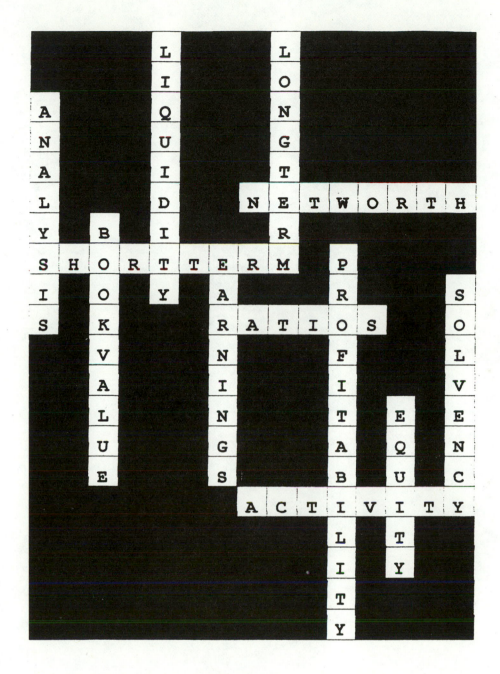

CHAPTER TWELVE

FINANCIAL STATEMENT ANALYSIS
An Introduction

EXERCISES

Ex. 1   Vocabulary review—listed below are many of the terms discussed in this chapter. Match these terms to their correct definitions given below.

a. Stockholders
b. Liquidity
c. Solvency
d. Activity ratios
e. Management
f. Profitability

g. Ratio analysis
h. Financial statement analysis
i. Short-term creditors
j. Long-term creditors
k. Liquidity ratios
l. Solvency ratios

_____ 1. The ease with which assets may be converted into cash.

_____ 2. People who have an ownership interest in a corporation.

_____ 3. Those who are charged with everyday operation of a company.

_____ 4. Financial lending institutions and bondholders.

_____ 5. Trade accounts payables and some lending institutions.

_____ 6. Analyzing numbers on financial statements into comparisons.

_____ 7. Measures the ease with which a company generates income.

_____ 8. Compares two amounts with each other from financial statements.

_____ 9. The ability of a company to generate cash for short-term debt.

_____10. The ability of a company to pay its long-term debt.

_____11. The efficiency with which the company's assets are used.

_____12. Looks at the overall debt and interest payments of a company.

Ex. 2.   Listed below are some of the ratios discussed in this chapter. Match the definitions given below to the appropriate ratio.

a.   Current ratio
b.   Total liabilities to net worth
c.   Profit margin before income taxes
d.   Return on assets
e.   Asset turnover
f.   Book value per share

g.   Earnings per share
h.   Inventory turnover
i.   Accounts receivable turnover
j.   Return on equity
k.   Coverage ratio
l.   Debt ratio
m.   Quick ratio

_____ 1.   Shows the return earned on total asset investment.

_____ 2.   The ability of equity investments to produce income.

_____ 3.   Measures the ability of the company to meet short-term obligations.

_____ 4.   Indicates the ability of the company to make its interest payments.

_____ 5.   A more restrictive measurement of the ability of a company to meet its short-term obligations.

_____ 6.   The relationship of debt financing to equity financing.

_____ 7.   Measures the efficiency with which assets generate sales.

_____ 8.   The ability of a company to collect the money owed to it.

_____ 9.   The amount of net income earned for each outstanding share of common stock.

_____10.   How long items of inventory remain in stock.

_____11.   The amount each share of common stock would receive if liquidation of the company took place.

_____12.   Measures the income produced at a certain level of sales.

_____13.   Measures the amount of assets financed by debt.

Ex. 3 Identify each of the ratios given below as either calculated for profitability (P), liquidity (L), activity (A), or solvency (S).

_____ 1. Total liabilities to net worth

_____ 2. Inventory turnover

_____ 3. Return on assets

_____ 4. Debt ratio

_____ 5. Accounts receivable turnover

_____ 6. Book value per share

_____ 7. Current ratio

_____ 8. Quick ratio

_____ 9. Coverage ratio

_____10. Return on equity

_____11. Net sales to working capital

_____12. Return before interest expense on equity

_____13. Total asset turnover

_____14. Total liabilities to net worth

_____15. Earnings per share

Ex. 4. A study of the comparative analysis for the past five years of Miles Delivery Company has revealed the following information about its current and quick ratios.

	1993	1994	1995	1996	1997
Current ratio	1.4	1.9	2.6	3.8	4.0
Quick ratio	1.3	1.0	.9	.7	.4

a. What has happened to the liquidity of Miles Delivery Service over the last 5 years?

b. What has happened to the makeup of the current assets over the last 5 years?

Ex. 5. A study of the comparative analysis for the past five years of Miles Delivery Company has revealed the following information about its total liabilities to net worth and its debt ratios.

	1993	1994	1995	1996	1997
Total liabilities to net worth	2.6	2.4	2.1	1.4	1.0
Debt ratio	70.0	68.7	65.1	61.3	52.3

a. What has happened to the capital makeup in Miles Delivery Company over the past five years?

b. Which users of financial statement analysis information would probably be most interested in this information?

Ex. 6.   Using the following information obtained from the income statement and balance sheet of Miles Delivery Company, calculate the results for the ratios listed below:

INCOME STATEMENT INFORMATION:

Revenue from Sales:	$12,000
Cost of Goods Sold:	8,000
Gross Profit from Sales:	$4,000
Less Total Operating Expenses	2,500
Net Income before Interest and Interest:	$1,500
Deduct Interest Expense:	400
Net Income before Taxes	$1,100
Deduct Income Taxes	500
Net Income	$ 600

BALANCE SHEET INFORMATION:

Current Assets:		
Cash	$1,600	
Accts. Receivable	1,900	
Merchandise Inven.	1,000	
Prepaid Insurance	200	
Total Current Assets		$4,700
Total Fixed Assets:		$6,000
Total Assets:		$10,700
Total Current Liabilities:		$2,700
Total Fixed Liabilities:		$2,400
Total Liabilities:		$5,100
Stockholder's Equity:		
Common Stock, No Par		
500 shares outstanding		$3,500
Retained Earnings		2,100
Total Stockholder's Equity:		$5,600
Total Liabil. + Stock. Equity		$10,700

(Continued)

CALCULATE THE FOLLOWING RATIOS:

a. Current ratio
b. Quick ratio
c. Earnings per share
d. Book value per share
e. Return on assets
f. Coverage ratio
g. Debt ratio
h. Total liabilities to net worth

i. Profit margin before taxes
j. Total asset turnover
k. Return on equity
l. Net sales to working capital
m. Accounts receivable turnover
n. Mdse. inventory turnover

Ex. 7. Obtain a copy of the annual stockholder's report for a company of your choice. Using the information that it provides, calculate the same ratios as you did for exercise 6.

WORKPAPER FOR EXERCISES

WORKPAPER FOR EXERCISES

WORKPAPER FOR EXERCISES